THE ANATOMY OF PEACE

By the Same Author

A DEMOCRATIC MANIFESTO

THE
ANATOMY
OF PEACE

BY
EMERY REVES

THE ANATOMY OF PEACE

Special edition published by the
Dallas Symphony Association, Inc.
Commemorating the gift of
Wendy Reves
In memory of her beloved husband
Emery Reves

THIS BOOK

IS DEDICATED TO THE

MEMORY OF MY MOTHER

who was atrociously and senselessly

assassinated, like countless other in-

nocent victims of the war whose

martyrdom can have meaning only

if we who survive learn

how to prevent the tragedy

of future wars.

CONTENTS

THE ANATOMY OF PEACE

CHAPTER I

A COPERNICAN WORLD

NOTHING can distort the true picture of conditions and events in this world more than to regard one's own country as the center of the universe, and to view all things solely in their relationship to this fixed point. It is inevitable that such a method of observation should create an entirely false perspective. Yet this is the only method admitted and used by the seventy or eighty national governments of our world, by our legislators and diplomats, by our press and radio. All the conclusions, principles and policies of the peoples are necessarily drawn from the warped picture of the world obtained by so primitive a method of observation.

Within such a contorted system of assumed fixed points, it is easy to demonstrate that the view taken from each point corresponds to reality. If we admit and apply this method, the viewpoint of every single nation appears indisputably correct and wholly justified. But we arrive at a hopelessly confused and grotesque over-all picture of the world.

Let us see how international events between the two world wars look from some of the major national vantage points.

The United States of America, faithful to the Monroe Doctrine and to its traditions of aloofness from Europe, did not want to enter the first World War. But the Germans were sinking American ships, violating American rights and threatening American interests. So in 1917, the United States was forced to go to war in defense of American rights. They went into battle determined to fight the war to end all war, and to "make the world safe for democracy." They fought bravely and spent lavishly. Their intervention decided the outcome of the struggle in favor of the Allies. But as soon as the shooting was over, the major Allied powers—Britain, France, Italy and Japan— betrayed the common cause. They were unwilling to base the peace on Wilson's ideals. They signed secret treaties between themselves. They did not want a just peace. They wanted to annex territories, islands, bases; they wanted to impose high reparation payments on the defeated countries and other measures of vengeance. America, disgusted by the quarrels and selfishness of the other nations and disillusioned by the old game of power politics, retired from the European hornet's nest, after having been abused, outsmarted and double-crossed by her former associates. America wanted only to be allowed to mind her own business, to build up the wealth and happiness of her own citizens. The foreign nations—who would have been crushed without American intervention and who were saved by America—even defaulted on their war debts and refused to repay the loans America had made to them in their hour of danger. So even financial and economic relations with the European powers had to be reduced to a minimum and American capital had to be protected by prohibiting loans to defaulting foreigners. American policy was fully justified by the ensuing events. Clouds were again gathering in Europe. Military dictatorships were arising in many countries, a race of armaments had started, violence broke out and the whole continent was on the verge of another great war—more of the old European quarrels and power politics. Naturally, it was of primary interest to the United States to keep out of these senseless internecine old-world fights. The supreme duty of the American government to its people was to maintain strict neutrality toward the warring nations across the ocean. Thanks to the weakness of the appeasement policy and the blindness of Britain, France and Soviet Russia, the totalitarian powers succeeded in conquering the entire European continent. German troops occupied the whole Atlantic seacoast from Norway to Equatorial Africa. Simultaneously, the Japanese succeeded in conquering the entire Chinese coastline, menacing the American-controlled Philippine Islands. Incredible and unbelievable as it was, no one could fail to see that the European and Asiatic military powers, known as the Axis, were planning the conquest of North and South America. In sheer self-defense, America was obliged to transform herself into the arsenal of democracy, producing weapons for the British and Russians to fight the Germans. Then, on a day which will "live in infamy" the Japanese Empire launched an unprovoked aggression against peace-loving America and, together with Germany and Italy, declared war upon her. Once forced into the war, the nation arose as one man. In a short time, it became obvious that once again the United States was saving the civilized Western world. Events have demonstrated that disarmament and disinterestedness cannot protect America from foreign aggression. Therefore, peace in the world can be preserved only if the United States maintains a large army, the biggest navy and the biggest air force in the world, and secures bases at all strategic points commanding the approaches to the Western Hemisphere.

How do these same twenty years look from the fixed point of the *British Isles?*

In 1914, Britain went to the defense of Belgium, France and Russia. It was impossible for her to stand by while militarist Germany was marching to occupy and control the Channel coast. Britain could not permit Germany to obtain European hegemony and to become the dominating industrial and military power on the Continent, menacing the lifelines of the British Empire and threatening to reduce the British Isles to starvation and poverty. When, at the cost of tremendous efforts and the lives of more than one million of her sons, Britain, together with her allies, won victory, she naturally wanted to see German military might eliminated once and for all from the path of the

British Empire. It was only just that the German fleet be destroyed, that German colonies be annexed and that Germany be made to pay reparations. Unfortunately, the isolationists in America stabbed Wilson in the back and the United States deserted her allies. England remained alone to face the European problem. Without the United States and without the Dominions, she could not give the guarantees France demanded and had to be careful lest after victory over Germany, France should take the place of the defeated Reich and become an overwhelmingly dominating military power on the Continent. As the French went berserk, refusing to disarm and occupying the Ruhr, England had to become the moderator in Europe and to continue the traditional balance-of-power policy that had been successful for so many centuries. Bolshevik Russia, after the failure of military intervention supported by the Allies, succeeded in stabilizing a Communist regime, and through the Third Internationale and the various Communist parties in Europe, threatened the entire Continent with revolution. Germany, suffering under the consequences of defeat and French intransigence, with six million unemployed, was particularly susceptible to revolutionary turmoil. It was of paramount importance for European peace that German economy be restored and stabilized. Mussolini had succeeded in reestablishing order in Italy and the growing strength of the National Socialist movement in Germany seemed to stem the tide of Bolshevism.

But Great Britain's economic problems were becoming aggravated. The Americans erected high tariff walls and refused to import British goods, thus making it impossible for Great Britain to repay her war debts. She was forced to give up her traditional free trade policy and to enter into a preference system with the Dominions. Italian and German intentions by this time began to alarm France and the smaller countries of Europe. Two camps began to crystallize, one trying to preserve the *status quo* of the Treaty of Versailles, the other seeking revisions favorable to them. Then as now peace was England's paramount interest and her natural role was to be the mediator between the two factions, to attempt as many revisions as possible by peaceful means so as to check the dynamism of the dictatorships, and to prevent an outbreak of hostilities at any cost. When Italy embarked upon her unfortunate military operation in Ethiopia, England championed the principles of the League. Sanctions were voted and imposed upon the aggressor by more than fifty nations under British leadership. It was a most alarming factor that France, frightened by growing German power and in the hope of obtaining Italian assistance against Germany in Europe, gave Italy a free hand in Ethiopia. So the League was sabotaged by France. Italy could not be stopped except by intervention of the British fleet, which would have meant risking a major war and had to be avoided. Shortly after the Italian conquest of Ethiopia, Germany reoccupied the

Rhineland. France, in her first reaction, wanted to march, but England prevented a military clash between the two major continental powers. For the pacification of Europe, an agreement was made with Germany granting her a new fleet, thirty-five per cent of the British tonnage. Thereafter, Germany and Italy formed a military alliance and provoked a civil war in Spain to try out new weapons and new methods of warfare, and to establish a regime friendly to them. This incident created a highly charged atmosphere all over Europe. Russians were actually fighting German and Italian forces on Spanish soil. Only by pursuing the strictest policy of nonintervention and exercising the utmost patience was England able to prevent France from intervening and spreading the fight all over the Continent. In the face of these threatening events, England succeeded in strengthening her ties with France. Unhappily, still further sacrifices had to be made to prevent a war, which England could not risk, as she was almost completely unprepared. Other adjustments of the territorial status of Europe had to be considered. At Munich, British diplomacy was taxed to the utmost to obtain the transfer of German-inhabited Czechoslovak territories to the Reich without a violent conflict. Once again England had saved the peace. But after Munich, it was apparent that Germany had made up her mind to conquer Europe. England had to begin rearming and to look around for allies. Belgium and Holland, jealous of their neutrality, did not admit military discussions, but the alliance with France was strengthened, alliances with Poland and Rumania were signed and every effort was made to reach an understanding with the Soviet Union. The Poles, however, stubbornly refused to permit Russian troops passage across Polish territory in case of war and in the middle of negotiations in Moscow, a diplomatic bomb exploded. Russia, betraying her Western democratic friends, had signed a nonaggression pact with Nazi Germany. That gave Germany the green light to attack Poland. All this happened within a few days and England, honoring her pledged word, declared war upon Germany. It was impossible for Britain to bring military help to the Poles in time and Poland was defeated in a few weeks. British troops, however, were sent to France, the best-equipped army ever to cross the Channel. They, along with French soldiers, took their posts at the Belgian and German frontiers and waited for the German attack, believing the defense system they and their allies held to be impregnable. But Hitler, instead of opening an offensive against the Allies, attacked the peaceful and undefended neutral countries of Denmark and Norway. Britain immediately sent an expeditionary force to Narvik, which fought gallantly but which had to withdraw before overwhelming enemy forces supported by land-based planes. Shortly thereafter, the Germans made a frontal attack against the west, occupying neutral Holland and Belgium in a few days. They turned the Maginot Line and cracked the French defenses. The King of Belgium surrendered. Only some of the British troops could be evacuated from Dunkirk and other ports of France. All the equipment of the British Expeditionary Force was lost. France, inadequately equipped and undermined by Nazi propaganda, betrayed her British ally by refusing to continue the fight on the side of the British Commonwealth in the Mediterranean and in Africa, and capitulated to Germany. The whole Continent was in German hands and England stood alone. The situation seemed hopeless. England was without defenses. The Luftwaffe began to bomb London and British industrial centers. Italy began to move against Egypt and Suez. Both the mother country and the lifeline of the empire in the Middle East were in mortal danger. Britain could have saved her empire had she accepted German hegemony in Europe, but she preferred to fight all alone, even if she had to fight on her beaches, on her hills and in her villages. Along with the sacrifice of tens of thousands of civilians, she won the Battle of Britain, fought off the Luftwaffe with a few fighter planes, fought the German submarines singlehanded, mobilized her entire population and dispatched everything she could to the Near East to stem Mussolini's advancing armies. For more than a year, Britain alone defended the cause of democracy. Neither the Soviet Union nor the United States was prepared to enter the war on her side. Only when Germany actually attacked Russia and Japan bombed Pearl Harbor and invaded the Philippines did Russia and the United States join forces with the British Commonwealth to achieve final victory.

From the point of view of *France,* the picture looked like this:

In 1914, France suffered the second German invasion within half a century. The entire north and east of France were devastated and only by tremendous bloodshed and the sacrifice of a million and a half of her sons could France defend her soil. With the help of the Allies, Germany was finally defeated. The supreme thought in the mind of every Frenchman was to be secure against another German aggression. France felt strongly that as the bastion of Western democracy she was entitled to security, to prevent her soil becoming the permanent battlefield of Teutonic aggression. To obviate the constant threat of Germans on the west bank of the Rhine, France demanded the Rhine as the new Franco-German border. Further, she demanded that Germany be demilitarized and forced to make reparation for the damage caused to France. At the peace conferences, however, she was abandoned by the United States and even to some extent by England and was obliged to accept a compromise. After having yielded to Anglo-American pressure she asked the United States and Britain to guarantee her eastern frontiers against German revenge. They refused. With a population much smaller than Germany, with a stationary birth rate in the face of Germany's increasing population, France had to rely on her own armed strength and on what alliances she could make with the newly created, smaller states east and south of Germany. When the Reich began to sabotage reparation payments, France, standing on her rights, occupied the Ruhr, but was not supported by her allies. After America had withdrawn from Europe into isolation, France did her utmost to support the League of Nations and, with her smaller allies, suggested a mutual assistance pact within the League—the Geneva Protocol. Britain refused to commit herself. France found a substitute in the Locarno agreements which at least guaranteed security in the West. From the threat of reborn German militarism in the form of Nazism, she vainly sought protection from England and finally turned to Italy whose interest regarding the prevention of the Austrian Anschluss was identical with that of France. But Italy abused France's gesture and attacked Ethiopia, in violation of her obligations to the League. France was in a desperate position between the League and Mussolini, and in the end lost the friendship of Italy to uphold the League. When the Germans remilitarized the Rhineland, France was alarmed and called upon her partners in the Locarno Pact, but they turned a deaf ear and she had to accept the German *fait accompli*. Feeling abandoned and growing weaker in the face of rapidly increasing German military power, France sought an alliance with Russia but was hindered by Poland who, although allied with France, would not give Russian troops permission to march through Polish territory. When Germany

and Italy fomented and supported the Franco
military revolution against the Spanish Republic,
it was obviously a move to encircle France. This
maneuver foreboded grave events. France wanted
to intervene on the republican side and thus prevent Franco, supported by Hitler and Mussolini,
from coming to power. But England opposed such
a move. So the French Republic had to stand by
and watch a hostile Fascist power being established by her enemies on her third land frontier.
She had staked everything on her friendship with
Britain. When it was obvious that Germany had
become the dominating military and industrial
power in Europe and that none of the other great
powers, neither the United States nor Britain nor
Russia, realized the imminence of danger, many
Frenchmen felt that to oppose German might
singlehanded was a suicidal policy, that the French
must resign themselves to German supremacy in
Europe and accept the position of a secondary
power on the Continent. France's internal stability
was greatly imperiled by a violent cleavage between capital and labor, and differences of opinion
between those who advocated a French policy of
collaboration with England and Russia and those
who sought an arrangement with Germany. In
spite of these difficulties, France kept faith with
her British ally and continued to follow her lead.
She accepted Munich, sacrificing Czechoslovakia,
her most faithful friend on the Continent. Her
armies were mobilized several times to be in readiness at critical moments. And when even Russia

abandoned her, signing a treaty with Germany, and Hitler attacked Poland, France fulfilled her obligation toward her Polish ally, despite the difficulties and disappointments created by the pro-German Polish policy of the previous years. France declared war on Germany, mobilized six million men and exposed herself to the inrush of Nazi military might. She urged Britain to send strong forces across the Channel but England sent only two or three hundred thousand men and when the Germans attacked in the west, France had to carry the burden of fighting practically alone. The King of Belgium laid down arms. The entire British Expeditionary Force was encircled and pushed into the sea at Dunkirk. The German Panzer divisions swept across all the northern departments of France with overwhelming force. In this critical moment, Italy stabbed France in the back and declared war. The military situation was hopeless. France appealed to America for help which was refused. The British withdrew, betraying their alliance with France in her darkest hour. There was no alternative but to accept the bitter humiliation of defeat and surrender, hoping for a miracle of resurrection and trying to accommodate France to the new order in Europe, to ease the suffering of her people. For four years, the French endured German occupation and helplessly watched the Nazis looting the country. They organized a heroic resistance movement both inside and outside France and four years later, after America had been forced into the war by Germany and

Japan, when the Anglo-American troops landed on French beaches, French resistance forces from outside came with them, and French resistance armies within the country arose, liberating their cities and villages, and contributing considerably to the Allied victory.

The image of these same events during the same period appeared to the *German* people as follows:

For more than four years from 1914 to 1918 the German armies fought a coalition of almost the entire world, which had refused Germany the place under the sun her growing population required. In spite of their numerical superiority, the Allies never defeated the German armies in battle but they did succeed in blinding a section of the German people with promises of a just peace so that pacifists, socialists, democrats and Jews at home revolted and stabbed the German armies in the back. At Versailles, Germany was unjustly accused of having been responsible for the war. The Allies imposed upon her a treaty based on this lie which meant the dismemberment and enslavement of the German people. Nevertheless, Germany signed this shameful treaty and did her utmost to fulfill its terms and to reestablish a friendly relationship with her former enemies, believing in their promises to disarm. Germany herself was disarmed and her people toiled in utmost poverty and misery to fulfill their obligation, toward the victors. On a pretext, France occupied the Ruhr, Germany's center of industrial production, establishing a regime of terror to enforce the unfulfillable clauses of the treaty. German economic life was disrupted and the country was plunged into an inflation which destroyed all the savings of the German population. Yet Germany accepted the Locarno treaties, guaranteeing once and for all her western frontiers, and entered the League. Germany signed the Kellogg Pact and outlawed war as an instrument of national policy. She insisted that the other parties keep their promises to disarm but they refused to do so. The chains of the Versailles Treaty became unbearable. The Allied powers refused to give Germany equality, a fair share in world trade, colonies and markets in central and southern Europe. Unemployment grew and misery reached unprecedented depths. Communism was spreading and it looked as if Germany would disintegrate, the German people be enslaved forever. During these desperate years, a savior arose who filled the German people with new hope, rallied them to his banner and promised work, bread, progress, strength for resurrection. The German people, by their own will power, liberated themselves from the chains of the Versailles Treaty, restored their own sovereignty by remilitarizing the German Rhineland. As the Allied powers refused to disarm and broke their own pledges, Germany regarded the military clauses of the treaty as null and void and began to assert her own dignity and to rearm. It was impossible for sixty-five million people to live in such a small and poor country. They needed living space if peace was to be preserved. The separation of German Austria from the Reich was ended and the German peoples were at last united. The new Germany gave work to everybody, spread wealth and happiness in the land and created a prosperity, a period of building and construction, unprecedented in German history. The German nation could not tolerate the spreading of Bolshevism in Europe and at great sacrifice helped the Spanish people to exterminate this Asiatic threat. As Germany arose from her defeat and was again a great, independent power, she could no longer admit the intolerable oppression and persecution of her blood brethren in Czechoslovakia. Relying on the righteousness of her cause, she claimed incorporation of the Sudeten German territories in the Reich which the former enemies of Germany were made to accept without force. But the enemies of peace had learned nothing. The Poles refused to stop oppressing and torturing German minorities and to allow their return to the German Reich. So Germany, to protect and defend her peoples, was forced to act. To prove her pacific intentions, she signed a treaty of nonaggression with Soviet Russia and liberated the lost German territories in the East. England and France, who for a long time were jealously watching Germany's resurrection, took advantage of her pacification of the East and declared war on the Reich without any provocation and with the clear intention of once again destroying and enslaving the German people. Germany had no quarrel with her western neighbors. So, although the Western world was fully mobilized and menaced German soil, Germany did not undertake any action but waited in the hope of a reasonable settlement with England and France. A few months later, however, it was obvious that England was planning to violate Danish and Norwegian neutrality in order to outflank German defenses from the north. The Wehrmacht had to intervene and protect the neutrality of Denmark and Norway. Shortly thereafter, British invasion of Belgium and Holland and the outflanking of the Westwall was threatening. No more time could be wasted. Germany had to strike in self-defense. The Wehrmacht attacked and in a few days achieved the greatest military victory of all times. Belgium and Holland were occupied, the British pushed back into the sea and France was brought to capitulation. In Compiègne, the Fuehrer avenged once and for all the German humiliation of 1918. Again Germany appealed to England to save the peace of the world, guaranteeing the integrity of the British Empire in exchange for British recognition of German *Lebensraum* in Europe. Britain stubbornly refused and began to bomb German cities in violation of civilized warfare. Germany was forced to retaliate. She had to strike at British harbors and military targets and to stop deliveries of arms to England by torpedoing British convoys. The Anti-Comintern Pact, which united the anti-Bolshevik forces of the new order, and the

German-Russian nonaggression pact, kept peace in the East. But intelligence reports made it more and more obvious that Soviet Russia was using the Russo-German pact merely to gain time and was secretly arming to the utmost of her ability. Russia was making preparations for an attack on Germany at a moment most convenient for her. Naturally, Germany could not expose herself to such mortal danger. She had to forestall Bolshevik treachery. With a lightning decision—characteristic of the intuition of the Fuehrer—Germany, in self-defense, struck at her foe. Her armies marched against the Soviet Union in order to prevent Bolshevik aggression and to destroy the Red Army, the greatest threat to European civilization...

And from the vantage point of *Moscow,* the same quarter century appeared in this light:

In 1917, the Russian people succeeded in overthrowing the autocratic dynasty which had oppressed and enslaved them for centuries, and established a socialist people's republic. The capitalist powers, the allies of czarist Russia, intervened militarily. America, England, France, Poland, sent troops into Russia to destroy the new republic and to reestablish the old regime of exploitatior.. The rapidly organized Red Army fought heroically, defeated the invaders and liberated the Russian soil. However, the young Soviet forces were not yet strong enough to push the armies of the capitalist imperialists back to the prewar frontier and so the Soviet government, in order to secure peace the quickest possible way, accepted a settlement which meant a loss of Russia's Baltic and western provinces. In spite of this settlement imposed on the Russian people, the hostility of the outside world toward the socialist experiment of the Soviet Union continued. Russia finally emerged from her involuntary isolation after five years by signing a treaty in Rapallo with the other prostrate power, Germany. Russia needed machinery, tools, engineers, to build up her industries and to raise the material conditions of her peoples, and Germany was prepared to do business with her. The Soviet Union bought everything for cash and paid in gold, so very soon England and America also began to sell their products in exchange for Russian gold. But the U.S.S.R. did not succeed in breaking the political hostility of the capitalist world. It became more and more obvious that the success of the Communist economic system aroused great apprehensions abroad and that the capitalist, imperialist countries would attack and destroy the Soviet Union at the earliest opportunity. All the neighboring countries —Finland, the Baltic States, Poland, Rumania, Turkey, the British Empire, Japan—were openly defying the Soviet Union and following an anti-Soviet policy. So Russia had to postpone her great plan to produce consumer goods in mass quantities and was forced by circumstances to build up key industries in order to construct factories for armament production, and to organize a land army and an air force of huge proportions to defend the Union. The more powerful the

U.S.S.R. became, the more resentment and animosity grew in capitalist countries. The friends of the Soviet people, the Communists, were persecuted everywhere. A new type of military imperialism, Fascism, was seizing power in one country after the other, intent upon destroying socialist Russia. When Fascism came into power in Germany and mobilized the great German industrial potential for war against Russia, the Soviet government tried to come to an agreement with the Western democratic nations who were also threatened by the growing German militarism. The Soviet Union entered the League of Nations and worked with all her might for the establishment of a system of collective security, for a system of alliances of the peace-loving nations, to make peace indivisible and to check aggression collectively whenever and wherever it started. Soon a Fascist aggression occurred. Italy attacked Ethiopia. But all the powers hesitated, temporized and appeased the aggressor, leaving Russia isolated in her fight for collective security. For several years, the Soviet Union passionately continued trying to organize the world for peace, advocating co-operation of the democratic, socialist and Communist forces in all countries to keep Fascism from spreading and to prevent aggression. America was inaccessible. England and France clearly did not want to align themselves formally with Soviet Russia against the Fascist forces. It became increasingly apparent that they would welcome a Fascist attack on the Soviet Union, that they would like to see the German people and their satellites engaged with the Soviet people in a long and bloody struggle. The Soviet government, desiring peace and knowing how disastrous such a war would be for the Soviet people, watched these maneuvers and manifestations of ill will with growing apprehension. They did their utmost to persuade the Western democracies of the suicidal shortsightedness of their policy. Finally, when Munich came and Britain and France, without even consulting the Soviet Union, sacrificed Czechoslovakia on the altar of appeasement, and permitted the destruction of the most valuable military link between Russia and the West, the situation became acute. A decision had to be made. Britain and France were invited to Moscow for conferences, but they sent only third-rate negotiators, affronting the Soviet government. Those negotiations left no doubt that even then, the Western powers did not desire wholehearted collaboration with Russia. They accepted the point of view of the Polish Fascists who refused to grant the Red Army permission to advance to the Polish-German border to organize common defenses. Then and there, it was clear that the arrangement suggested to the Soviet Union by the Western powers had no practical meaning and that it would inevitably result in a clash between the German and Russian armies with terrible bloodshed and serious consequences for the Soviet Union. To prevent such a catastrophe, the Soviet government had to make a decision. A radical change had to be made in past policy. They accepted a German proposal for a nonaggression pact which guaranteed the Soviet frontiers and peace, at least for a certain time, between the German Reich and the U.S.S.R. After signing the pact, the German armies attacked Poland. The Polish armies—on which the Western powers had wanted to base their entire Eastern defenses—collapsed in a few days. The Polish state ceased to exist. To prevent the Nazi militarists from reaching the Soviet borders, Red Army units reoccupied the lands inhabited by Ukrainians and White Russians which had been stolen from them by Poland during the revolution when the Soviet Union was weak. Through this act of foresight the German armies were stopped at a safe distance from the heart of Russia, and the Anti-Comintern Pact, the alliance between Germany, Japan and their satellites, against the Soviet Union was neutralized. Shortly after, Soviet diplomacy was justified when Germany attacked the West, defeating the French and British armies, and established Nazi hegemony over the entire European Continent, except the Soviet Union. One year later, the German Fascists unmasked their aggressive imperialism. Hitler violated his pact with Moscow and attacked the Soviet Union. By that time, however, the Russian armies were in readiness and defense industries were working to full capacity far behind the front lines. As a result of German aggression against the Soviet Union, the U.S.S.R. became the ally of the British Empire and later, of the United States. All these tragic events prove how correct was Russia's foreign policy, how justified her admonitions to the democratic world in the prewar years. But they also show that the U.S.S.R. must constantly be alert and prepared in the face of intrigues and aggressions of any of the foreign countries. In a world of hostile powers, the Soviet Union will have to maneuver between them and accept the alliances of those who will align themselves with her against the power or powers which represent the most imminent danger to the Soviet motherland.

The dramatic and strange events between the two world wars could be just as well described from the point of view of any other nation, large or small. From Tokyo or Warsaw, from Riga or Rome, from Prague or Budapest, each picture will be entirely different and, from the fixed national point of observation, it will always be indisputably and unchallengeably correct. And the citizens of every country will be at all times convinced—and rightly so—of the infallibility of their views and the objectivity of their conclusions.

It is surely obvious that agreement, or common understanding, between different nations, basing their relations on such a primitive method of judgment, is an absolute impossibility. A picture of the world pieced together like a mosaic from its various national components is a picture that never and under no circumstances can have any relation to reality, unless we deny that such a thing as reality exists.

The world and history cannot be as they appear to the different nations, unless we disavow objectivity, reason and scientific methods of research.

But if we believe that man is, to a certain degree, different from the animal and that he is endowed with a capacity for phenomenological thinking, then the time has come to realize that our inherited method of observation in political and social matters is childishly primitive, hopelessly inadequate and thoroughly wrong. If we want to try to create at least the beginning of orderly relations between nations, we must try to arrive at a more scientific, more objective method of observation, without which we shall never be able to see social and political problems as they really are, nor to perceive their incidence. And without a correct diagnosis of the disease, there is no hope for a cure.

Our political and social thinking today is passing through a revolutionary era very much the same as were astronomy and abstract science during the Renaissance.

For more than fourteen centuries, the geocentric theory of the universe, formulated and laid down by Ptolemy in the second century A.D. in Alexandria, was paramount in the scientific world. According to this theory—as explained in Ptolemy's famous *Almagest,* the culmination of

Greek astronomy—the earth was the center of the universe around which revolved the sun, the moon and all the stars.

No matter now primitive such a conception of the universe appears to us today, it remained unchallenged and unchallengeable for fourteen hundred years. All possible experimentation and observation before the sixteenth century A.D. confirmed the Ptolemaic system as a rock of indisputable scientific truth.

Strangely enough, Greek scientists several centuries before Ptolemy had a concept of the universe far more advanced and nearer to our modern knowledge. As far back as the sixth century B.C., Pythagoras visualized the earth and the universe as being spherical in shape. One of his later disciples, Aristarchus of Samos, in the third century B.C., in his hypothesis deposed the earth as the center of the universe, and declared it to be a "planet," like the many other celestial bodies. This system, called the Pythagorean system, plainly anticipated the Copernican hypothesis nineteen centuries later. It was probably not completely developed by Pythagoras himself, but it had been known several hundred years before Ptolemy.

Yet for almost two thousands years following the first insight into the real construction and functioning of the universe, people were convinced that all the celestial bodies revolved around the earth, which was the fixed center of the universe.

The geocentric system worked perfectly as long

as it could solve all the problems which presented themselves under the then existing methods of observation. Ptolemy himself appears to have sensed and suspected the transitory character of his system, as in his *Syntaxis* he laid down the general principle that in seeking to explain phenomena, we should adopt the simplest possible hypothesis, *provided it is not contradicted in any important respect by observation.*

The geocentric theory of Ptolemy was perfectly in harmony with the religious dogma concerning the story of the creation of the universe as told in the Bible and it became the doctrine approved by the Church.

But in fifteenth century Italy, under the light of new learning and observation and under the impetus of the revolt against the dictatorship of accepted philosophical and scientific doctrines, there came a radical change. Several thinkers, particularly one Dominico Maria Novara, denounced the Ptolemaic system and began spreading "Pythagorean opinions"—as they were called—about the universe. Around 1500, these old, yet revolutionary ideas, attracted and deeply interested young Copernicus while he was studying at the universities of Bologna and Padua.

So new circumstances, new methods of observation, new needs, led to the birth of the Copernican system, one of the most gigantic steps of scientific progress in human history.

Through the Copernican system, man's outlook on the universe changed fundamentally. In this new concept, the earth itself rotated. It was no longer a stable point. Our globe, just like the other planets, revolved in space around the sun and the new theory of planetary movement was founded on the principle of relativity of motion.

This heliocentric theory of Copernicus was by no means perfect. It solved many problems the Ptolemaic system could not solve, but certain outstanding anomalies compromised its harmonious working. It is also well known that for thirty-five years Copernicus did not dare publicly proclaim his discovery. When he finally decided to publish it (in the year of his death) he called his theory "Hypothesis" to forestall the wrath of the Church and public opinion.

The later experience of Galileo proved how justified were the fears of Copernicus. The heliocentric theory was not only condemned by the church authorities as heresy; it was rejected by the greatest astronomers and other scientists of the time. Indeed, it was impossible to prove Copernicus' hypothesis by the then existing methods of observation. Only later, through the work of Kepler and Galileo, was the heliocentric theory put on a solid scientific foundation.

At its inception, the Copernican system was nothing more than a daring speculation. But it opened a new world, pointed out the road to science and prompted new and more refined methods of observation which finally led to general acceptance of the revolutionary but correct outlook on the universe.

During the first half of the twentieth century, in so far as our political, social and economic thinking is concerned, we find ourselves in the same dead-end road as Copernicus during the Jubilee of 1500.

We are living in a geocentric world of nation-states. We look upon economic, social and political problems as "national" problems. No matter in which country we live, the center of our political universe is our own nation. In our outlook, the immovable point around which all the other nations, all the problems and events outside our nation, the rest of the world, supposedly rotate, is—our nation.

This is our basic and fundamental dogma.

According to this nation-centric conception of world affairs, we can solve political, economic and social problems within our nation, the fixed, immutable center, in one way—through law and government. And in the circumambient world around us, in our relations with the peoples of other nations, these same problems should be treated by other means—by "policy" and "diplomacy."

According to this nation-centric conception of world affairs, the political, social and economic relations between man and man living within a sovereign national unit, and these very same relationships between man and man living in separate sovereign national units are qualitatively different and require two qualitatively different methods of handling.

For many centuries such an approach was unchallenged and unchallengeable. It served to solve current problems in a satisfactory way and the existing methods of production, distribution, of communications and of interchange among the nations did not necessitate nor justify the formulation and acceptance of a different outlook. But the scientific and technological developments achieved by the industrial revolution in one century have brought about in our political outlook and in our approach to political and social phenomena a change as inevitable and imperative as the Renaissance brought about in our philosophical outlook.

The developments creating that need are revolutionary and without parallel in human history. In one century, the population of this earth has been more than trebled. Since the very beginning of recorded history, for ten thousand years, communication was based on animal power. During the American and French revolutions, transportation was scarcely faster than it had been under the Pharaohs, at the time of Buddha or of the Incas. And then, after a static aeon of ten thousand years, transportation changed within a single short century from animal power to the steam and electric railroad, the internal combustion automobile and the six hundred-mile-per-hour jet propulsion plane.

After thousands of years of primitive, rural existence in which all human beings, with few exceptions, were exhausted from producing with their own hands just enough food, clothing and shelter for sheer survival, in less than one century the population of the entire Western world has become consumers of mass-production commodities.

The change created by industrialism is so revolutionary, so profound, that it is without parallel in the history of any civilization. Despite Spengler, it is unique.

In this new and as yet unexplored era we find ourselves completely helpless, equipped with the inadequate, primitive political and social notions inherited from the pre-industrialized world. Slowly we are coming to realize that none of our accepted theories is satisfactory to cope with the disturbing and complex problems of today.

We realize that although we can have all the machinery we need, we cannot solve the problems of production. We realize that in spite of the far-flung and tremendous scope of transportation, we cannot prevent famine and starvation in many places, while there is abundance elsewhere on the earth. We realize that although hundreds of millions are desperately in need of food and industrial products, we cannot prevent mass unemployment. We realize that even though we have mined more gold than ever before, we cannot stabilize currency. We realize that while every modern country needs raw materials that other countries have, and produces goods which other countries need, we have been unable to organize a satisfactory method of exchange. We realize that although the overwhelming majority of all people hate violence and long to live in peace, we cannot prevent recurrent and increasingly devastating world wars. We knew that armaments must lead to wars between nations, but we have learned the bitter truth that disarmament also leads to war.

In this confusion and chaos in which civilized nations are struggling with utter helplessness, we are bound to arrive at the inevitable conclusion that the cause of this hopelessness and helplessness lies not in the outer world but in ourselves. Not in the problems we have to solve but in the hypotheses with which we approach their solutions.

Our political and social conceptions are Ptolemaic.

The world in which we live is Copernican.

Our Ptolemaic political conceptions in a Copernican industrial world are bankrupt. Latest observations on ever-changing conditions have made our Ptolemaic approach utterly ridiculous and out-of-date. We still believe, in each one of the seventy or eighty sovereign states, that our "nation" is the immovable center around which the whole world revolves.

There is not the slightest hope that we can possibly solve any of the vital problems of our generation until we rise above dogmatic nation-centric conceptions and realize that, in order to understand the political, economic and social problems of this highly integrated and industrialized world, we have to shift our standpoint and see all the nations and national matters in motion, in their interrelated functions, rotating according to the same laws without any fixed points created by our own imagination for our own convenience.

PART ONE

CHAPTER II

FAILURE OF CAPITALISM

I N THE present turmoil of international relations, we hear nation accusing nation in a most peculiar way, the voice of each lifted against the others.

Fascist countries assert that democracy and Communism are one and the same thing, that democracy is only a political corollary of Communism, that a democratic system of government must lead to Bolshevism.

Communists insist that democracy and Fascism are one and the same thing, that both are capitalist, that under both, private capital exploits the workers, that Fascism is the latest and highest form of capitalism, nothing but a device of reactionaries to destroy socialism.

Democratic countries emphasize more and more frequently that Fascism and Communism are one and the same thing, that both are totalitarian dictatorships oppressing the peoples by means of a ruthless police, destroying all liberties and reducing the individual to the status of a serf.

A grain of truth can be found in each of these triangular cross-charges. But actually, each expresses a superficial and worthless point of view. Mankind is engaged in an unprecedented life and death struggle, in a world-wide civil war waged around these social, political and economic conceptions. If it is to survive, these vital issues must be clarified, these conflicting notions must be separated and defined objectively.

Individualist capitalism, the system of free enterprise and free competition, was the dominant economic philosophy at the birth of industrialism. At the beginning of the nineteenth century, when the industrial revolution began, the liberating political revolutions of the late eighteenth century had been consolidated, their aims achieved. Democratic nation-states, republics and constitutional monarchies, were firmly established in the Western world. It was only natural that the political ideals which had triumphed should also become the prevailing basic principles of the economists, manufacturers and traders of the early industrial age.

Free enterprise, free trade and free competition were the obvious economic corollary of political liberty. On the basis of these principles, Adam Smith, David Ricardo and John Stuart Mill constructed a system of economic laws, a doctrine unchallengeable in the abstract even today.

But there is a fundamental difference between political freedom as embodied in English common law and proclaimed by the encyclopedists of the French Revolution and the fathers of American Independence—and economic freedom as understood by the classical economists of the early nineteenth century.

The founders of modern political democracy understood that freedom in human society is relative, and that freedom in the absolute is bound to lead to anarchy, to violence—to the exact opposite of freedom. They realized that the freedom for which man had been struggling for five thousand years, means in practice only the proper regulation of the interdependence of individuals within a society. They saw that human freedom can be created only by limiting the free exercise of human impulses through generally applied compulsion—in other words, by law.

Freedom is an ideal that appeals to everyone. The only trouble is that one's own longing for freedom is somewhat upset by a similar longing for freedom in others. What slightly complicates the eternal problem of freedom is the not quite negligible fact that hundreds of millions of human beings are dominated by the same subjective desire—freedom—the full exercise of which by every one of the hundreds of millions of individuals would necessarily impinge upon the freedom of all others.

So it was obvious to the makers of modern democratic constitutions that freedom can be granted to an individual only to the extent that the freedom of action of one individual does not infringe upon the freedom of action of other individuals. Individual freedom, as granted by the constitutions of all modern democracies to the citizens, is clearly defined by law as a series of compulsions imposed upon all individuals by the community—the state.

The economists of *laissez-faire,* however, failed to conceive freedom in its only possible form—in the form of a synthesis between freedom of action, and the prohibition of such actions as might impair or destroy the freedom of others. Freedom in economic affairs, according to their theory, was absolute, unlimited and unrestrained.

They had a nebulous notion about the necessity of protecting the economic freedom of man from infringement by the actions of others, but compared with the clear principles regarding freedom in human society which guided the authors of the modern democratic constitutions, theirs were extremely primitive. They fought against monopoly tendencies, knowing that these would strangle competition. But their stand against restricting competition among laborers was based on the same argument, i.e., that such restrictions would destroy freedom of competition between workers, that what is today called "collective bargaining" on the part of organized workers would be unfair to nonorganized labor, to the consumers, and would produce unemployment. They did not realize that trade unionism was the specific reaction to the total lack of norms regulating the relationship between employer and employee, to the unregulated, absolute freedom on the labor market which was gradually destroying the freedom of the wage earners.

Absolute, unlimited and unrestrained freedom of action could bring about "freedom" in this world only if absolute equality in every respect existed between individuals, if an order could be established which everyone would consider just and if it were possible to preserve such order in static form forever—or at least for a long period of time. It is evident that such absolute equality among men does not and never can exist. Economic conditions, like life itself, are in a permanent state of flux, and so after a short time, absolute economic freedom, like absolute freedom in any other field, created a situation in which many, if not the majority of people, were in fact deprived of freedom.

An economic order could rightly be called a system of absolute free enterprise based on absolute freedom of competition if inheritance did not exist; if, at the death of each individual, all the tools, all the means of production and wealth he had accumulated during his lifetime were destroyed or taken by the state, so as to give each person complete equality of opportunity. As such a thing is not likely to come to pass, freedom of enterprise and freedom of opportunity can at best be relative.

Theoretically, complete freedom of competition in economic life is thinkable only if each person starts from scratch. The moment capital, business organization, tools, patents and other assets accumulated by successful individuals during their activity in the field of free competition, are transferred to other individuals, who thus start with a great advantage over many others of their generation, absolute freedom of competition loses its meaning. In such a situation, if complete tyranny by a few economic dynasties is to be prevented and a relative degree of freedom in economic life is to be maintained, a certain amount of regulation by law is imperative and unavoidable.

In human society it is difficult to challenge the righteousness and justification of the claim for leadership and privileged positions of those who are more capable, more diligent, more intelligent, more thrifty. But it became hard for the masses to accept justification of the claim for leadership and privileged positions of second or third generations who inherited fortunes and capital from their parents, thus starting upon free enterprise in economic life under conditions so favorable that free competition became a method of perpetuating economic inequalities.

We cannot very well call the order existing today in the United States, the British Commonwealth and in other capitalist countries a "system of free enterprise" when many industries are monopolized to an extent which makes it absolutely impossible to start new ventures in those fields or to compete with those industries.

Consequently, within two or three decades, modern industrialism has created not only hitherto undreamed-of wealth for the economically stronger and more fit, as well as for their descendants, but it has also created poverty, frustration, dependency and lack of freedom, bitterly resented by those millions who lost their chance to become independent and whose labor is now a mere commodity.

This situation naturally created reactions, and finally modern socialism.

Socialism teaches that private capitalism necessarily leads to monopoly—to a greater concentration of capital in the hands of the few, to economic dismemberment and to the pauperization of the laboring masses. The conception of class warfare between capitalists and proletariat was construed and the salvation of the Western industrial world was seen to lie in the expropriation of the exploiters, in the abolition of the profit motive and in the nationalization of all means of production.

For nearly a century now this class warfare has been going on in all Western countries, despite the fact that the entire controversy is based on a misconception. It is not because capital is controlled by individuals and private corporations that the private capitalist system of free enterprise failed. It failed because in the economic field, "freedom" was regarded as an absolute instead of a functional concept, a human ideal in constant need of adjustment and regulation by law, and of institutions for its defense and safeguard. In absolute form, freedom of one man means the serfdom of the other. Obviously such a state of affairs cannot be a human ideal and cannot be called "freedom."

After a period of fabulous wealth for a few and increasing poverty for many, some people recognized the danger of the trend and tried to bridge the abyss separating the capitalist and proletarian classes by accepting trade-unionism, introducing labor legislation, social security, inheritance taxes and other measures to overcome the most blatant injustices arising from absolute freedom in economic life. Experience with social legislation unquestionably demonstrates that in this direction lies the solution of the social problem. If freedom in economic life is to have meaning, we must create a system of regulations and norms within which free enterprise, free initiative and freedom of economic activity can exist without destroying the freedom of enterprise, free initiative and free economic activity of others. This principle cannot work realistically except by establishing institutions capable of giving expression to constantly changing conditions and of creating law.

The scope and limits of free enterprise are just as relative as are those of any other freedom in human society. It was not so long ago that raising armies came within the scope of private enterprise. Just as modern capitalist states own a few industrial enterprises, the state—the king—also had an army. But the king could not wage war without the support and collaboration of his great landowners, just as modern democratic states cannot wage war without the support and collaboration of the great industrial enterprises. And just as governments today call upon private industrialists to produce guns, planes and ships for them, in other days powerful knights were called upon to raise armed battalions and to take command over them.

It is not so long since the champions of absolute

free enterprise hotly defended their sacred right to raise and possess armies. Who today would defend that right and assume that private enterprise includes the right of the big landowner or the big employer to raise and command armies? Who today would regard state monopoly of conscription and of maintaining armed forces as an infringement upon the system of free enterprise? Or is the Duke of Atholl, who still enjoys the privilege of maintaining a private army in Scotland, the only remnant of the system of free enterprise in the Western world?

The fact that at certain stages, evolution demands the transfer of certain human activities from the individual to the collectivity does not mean the end of individualism. It means, rather, that the interest of the community and the freedom of its members are better served if certain activities vitally concerning all are under the control of the community.

From a dogmatic viewpoint of absolute individual free enterprise, it is difficult to speak of freedom of enterprise in America or in England, when no landowner, no banker, no industrialist, is free to raise armies and fight under his individual banner, for his own house, for his own interests, for his own independence. The state monopoly of conscription, of raising and maintaining armed forces, is such a far-reaching infringement upon absolute individual liberty and the system of absolute freedom of enterprise, that it outranks completely the limitations upon free enterprise arising from trade-unionism or social legislation. Yet, after a hard and long fight between the defenders of free military enterprise and the community, that issue has been settled so that today, no one, not even the most adventurous industrial robber baron, believes that his individual freedom of action has been destroyed and that he is living in a Communist society just because he is no longer free to invest capital in a private army.

Our civic life is based entirely on the fundamental doctrine that maximum individual freedom results from the prohibition of the free exercise of such human actions as would infringe upon the freedom of action of others. This is the meaning of political freedom.

It is also the meaning of economic freedom.

The first conflict between false theory and reality in the industrial age—the anarchic situation created by the erroneous conception of freedom in economic life—might have been solved, after many unnecessary struggles, by a *rapprochement* between capitalist and socialist doctrines through social legislation, as it has been very nearly solved in small, progressive countries like Sweden, Denmark and Norway. But an even greater barrier to free industrial development, a dominating force in our civilization, has created a much more violent conflict which threatens to destroy all the positive achievements of the past two centuries. This conflict is the clash between industrialism and political nationalism.

Modern industrial economy, in order to

progress, needs freedom of exchange and transportation even more than it needs freedom of
individual initiative and competition. The purpose
of mechanized industrial economy is maximum
production of consumer goods. This entails the
utmost rationalization of production processes,
widespread division of labor, plant location on the
economically most favorable geographic sites, free
supplies of raw materials from all over the earth
and free distribution of finished products to all
world markets. These conditions essential to industrial development were recognized at the beginning of the industrial age; and free trade became
the natural policy of the first great industrial
power, England, where abolition of the tariffs on
agricultural products—the remnants of the mer-
cantile age—was urged and complete freedom in
international trading advocated.

But by the time free trade had established England's leadership in industrial production and
world trade, the eighteenth century nation-state
system had already crystallized as a rigid political
structure. People in the Western world had begun
to think in national terms, pledging allegiance to
their nation-states, their national symbols and
ideals above everything else. And these young
nation-states—the United States, Germany,
France—looked with envy upon England's growing wealth created by her industrial power and
export trade. They began to feel that free trade
was a very profitable policy indeed for the economically strongest nation and that, under the

existing freedom of economic exchange they themselves had very little chance to build up industries at home, capable of competing with British manufacturers. They wanted to produce within their own national borders as much as possible of what they needed, and in addition, a substantial volume of commodities for export.

To create a national industry became more important to them than to carry on the free trade system, even if such a change of policy meant higher prices at home. Each felt that, as a national unit, it would have more "freedom" if it put legal restrictions on the freedom of trade of the stronger producer nations. So, championed by Alexander Hamilton and Friedrich List, a new theory of industrial protection was born and national tariff barriers were erected under the protection of which national industries came into being in the United States, in Germany and in various other countries.

From that moment, the system of free individualist economy—a most promising departure—was halted, disrupted and strangled.

Since the middle of the nineteenth century, it has been meaningless to talk of a free economy. The reality consists of a system of warring national economies guided primarily by political and not economic interests and considerations.

For a relatively short time—about half a century—this misalliance between industrialism and nationalism could be overlooked because in the politically divided world a few nations were

large enough for industrialism to continue to
develop. For a time sufficient open spaces provided conditions that enabled the relative wealth
of the United States and of the colonial powers of
Great Britain, France, Germany, Holland and Belgium to be created. All of these nations were engaged in desperate competition during the entire
nineteenth century, seeking to bring under their
own national sovereignty territories large enough
to supply their industrial machinery with raw
materials and markets of their own.

This development finally reached a saturation
point. Once there were no more territories to dis-
cover, once the possibility of annexing virgin lands
ceased, these divided national industrial states got
into violent collisions with each other, starting a
new type of conflict, creating more and more
chaotic conditions throughout the world.

Within narrow national boundaries fortified by
artificial tariff walls, economic freedom became a
farce. The impossibility of exchanging freely, of
producing where production was economically
most rational, of supplying the markets where a
demand for commodities existed, accelerated and
made more acute the periodical crises within the
system of national economies, bringing about
unemployment and misery in the midst of plenty.

What we usually call world economics, international trade, has today little, if anything, to do
with economics or trade. They are in fact economic warfare, trade warfare. The dominating
motive of all economic activity outside existing

national boundaries is not trade, is not production, is not consumption, is not even profit, but a determination to strengthen by all means the economic power of the nation-states.

Within the political strait-jacket of the nation-states, national economies could function only through artificial stimulants which, after a brief flurry, made the position even worse. Capitalists, who originally thought that they profited most by the system of free enterprise began to seek to eliminate competition, the very foundation of the capitalist system. Artificial structures, trusts and cartels, were erected to control competition and to circumvent the iron laws of supply and demand on the free market. They thought they saw salvation in economic planning, fixing in advance quality, quantity and rate of production to avoid overproduction and to keep prices high.

On the other hand, the workers, whose sufferings increased under this system of anarchic economy, rejected the very idea of private capital and free enterprise, organized trade unions to obtain higher wages through collective bargaining and formed political parties to influence legislation and control governments.

On all sides today in the Western world voices are raised accusing managers of trusts and cartels as well as the leaders of labor parties and trade unions of destroying individual freedom. The cry is that planned economy, whether controlled by capitalist cartels or socialist labor parties, inevitably leads to dictatorship and destruction of democracy.

This is unquestionably true.

Both cartels and labor unions have been driving the great industrial democracies of the Western world toward more government control and less individual freedom. But the strange thing is that none of these champions of absolute individual and economic liberty have taken the trouble to analyze the crisis through which the world is passing. None of them have tried to determine the underlying causes of the trend, nor the forces which are driving us toward ever-increasing power for the state. They assert it is the leaders of cartels with their fear of competition, and the socialists with their collectivist ideology, who cause this trend. Some are even so blind as to declare that no "objective facts" make inevitable our march toward complete state control. Only wrong ideas, only human stupidity, they say are responsible for the present situation which has come about because people "believe" in false prophets and in the heresies of economic planning, collectivism and government control.

Economic freedom and the system of free enterprise have been driven into bankruptcy by the primitive, erroneous notion of unregulated freedom and by political nationalism, by the nation-state structure.

Except for a limited period after the birth of industrialism, free economy has never really existed. The political credo of nationalism undermined and destroyed it before it could develop.

The primacy of national interests in every

country forces governments and peoples toward economic self-sufficiency, toward preparedness for war, toward more economic planning and direction, which means the transfer of more and more authority from individuals to the central government. The political structure of the nation-states is in violent and absolute opposition to the needs of an economic system of free enterprise. In final analysis, all obstacles to free economy arising in the democratic countries derive from it.

To all practical purposes it is today a waste of time to search for the laws of economic life. In a world of national industrialism, it is the gun that regulates production, trade and consumption. There is no higher law to govern economy in a world of sovereign nation-states.

Monopolistic tendencies, socialism, collectivism are merely reactions, attempts to cure the most urgent symptoms of the crisis created by the clash between industrialism and nationalism. Developments in every single nation-state have run parallel, albeit with varying rapidity, toward the domination of the individual by the state, first in his economic and then automatically in his political life.

From this evolution over the past fifty years, it is clear that individual capitalism, within the limited boundaries of nation-states at the present stage of industrial development, cannot operate without causing anarchic conditions that force governments to intervene and take control of the economic process in the interest of the nation. The advantages of a free economic system, higher living standards, greater wealth, better housing, better education, more leisure are unquestionable. But it remains a fact that they mean much less to the blind citizen-serfs of the nation-states, than their nationalist passions. People willingly and enthusiastically renounce the enjoyment of freedom and wealth, if only they can continue to indulge in slavish submission to and abject worship of their nation-state and its symbols.

The individual system of free enterprise within the limits of nation-states can neither flourish nor develop. In all countries it has led to more and more power for the state, to a totalitarian form of government and the destruction of individual liberty.

Prohibitive tariff walls, monopolies, cartels, control of government by trusts and private interests, dumping, poverty, slums, unemployment and many other products of the system of absolute free enterprise are surely not freedom, or freedom has no meaning.

CHAPTER III

FAILURE OF SOCIALISM

AFTER decades of unrest, struggle and attempted revolutions, in 1917 one great country at last became the scene of a large-scale socialist experiment—Russia. Contrary to the predictions of Marx, Communism first succeeded in establishing the dictatorship of the proletariat, not in the most advanced industrial country but in one of the most backward. This alone, in such contradiction to the Marxist timetable and theories, should have sufficed to arouse immediate suspicion as to the socialist quality of the Russian Revolution. Later developments have proved, and history will undoubtedly record the events of 1917 to be not so much a socialist revolution, as the Great Russian National Revolution, coming a hundred and fifty years after the national revolutions of the Western countries and creating not socialism but something quite different.

The slogans and the symbols that germinated the revolution are losing their meaning and importance in the light of more significant historic facts. In 1917, the main revolutionary force of the world was Communism, which unquestionably gave impetus to the violent overthrow of the old regime, czarism and capitalism alike. But the revolution did not establish economic equality and social justice, the aim of its originators. It brought about something quite different.

No doubt Lenin, Trotsky, Bukharin and the other theorists and initiators of the Russian Bolshevik revolution were idealists who sincerely believed in a Marxist collectivist society. They were convinced that once "ownership" of land and means of production were expropriated and transferred from private individuals and corporations to the collectivity, represented by the state, social equality would be achieved and a new, prosperous and happy society created. They resorted to terror only as a temporary measure to remove the parasites of the old regime. The dictatorship of the proletariat was to be merely a period of transition, as Marx taught, during which the expropriation of private capital and its transfer to the state was necessary, but would be abolished automatically as soon as the operation was completed and a classless society created.

A few years after the revolution, it became obvious, even to the Soviet leaders, that absolute economic and social equality are incompatible with the very nature of man, that private initiative is essential to progress and that a certain amount of property is an inevitable corollary to the conception of human liberty. A series of reforms were introduced to differentiate income and social position, which in a few years led to gradations in wealth, power and influence as pronounced as in any capitalist country.

One thing about the Soviet system, however,

was indisputable. It worked. In an economic system controlled entirely by the collectivity, the agricultural output was raised; coal, iron and gold were mined in ever-increasing quantities; huge factories, dams and railroads were built; steel, aluminum and textiles were produced; tractors, cars and airplanes were manufactured.

The complete failure of the Comintern ideal of world revolution as propagated by Trotsky, Zinoviev and the old guard of Lenin's disciples, strengthened the position of those who believed that the Soviet Union would perish if it entered into conflict with other nations, that it must be prepared to resist foreign aggression, that the Soviet peoples must concentrate on increasing the industrial strength of the U.S.S.R. rather than on spreading revolution.

For two decades the Russian people worked with all their energy and devotion to lay the foundation of a great industrial power and to produce the arms and munitions necessary to defend the sacred soil of their country against attack. But in spite of the fabulous production figures of Russian heavy industry, the standard of living of the great masses of the Russian people remained stagnant. Although they have expanded their system of transportation and opened up wide, undeveloped spaces for settlement, their standard of living has remained extremely low.

It does not detract one iota from the achievements of the Russian people to state that almost none of the social ideals of Marx and Lenin have been achieved in the Soviet Union through the dictatorship of the proletariat. The workers are living under material conditions less favorable than those in the Western democracies. Individual liberty is nonexistent. Although all natural resources and tools are collective property, the relationship between management and worker is in principle the same as in England or America— in practice, worse. Soviet labor unions are instruments of the state and can do little toward improving working conditions for their members. In any dispute, the management is just another instrument of the same state. Most of the workers are tied to the factory or mine or land where they work, and have no freedom of movement if dissatisfied with the existing surroundings and conditions. In a short span of twenty years, after the complete elimination of all upper and middle classes, a new ruling class has crystallized. A Red Army general, a high government official, a successful engineer or a famous writer, painter or orchestra conductor is just as far above the great masses of labor as in the most capitalist country.

Developments during the first twenty-five years of the first Communist state run surprisingly parallel to the evolution of capitalist democratic countries. In a state of permanent international distrust, under constant fear of foreign aggression, in perpetual danger of destruction by outside forces, under pressure of the political nation-state structure of the world, the first and foremost endeavor of the Soviet peoples was to strengthen the power of the centralized Soviet state. The survival, at all costs of the national state—the U.S.S.R.—is the dominant doctrine of the Stalin regime. It did not take long for the original internationalism in Communist philosophy to fade away and disappear, to give way to National Communism.

Since Stalin's victory over Trotsky, the Soviet government has been building up the industrial and military power of the U.S.S.R., forging the heterogeneous elements of that huge country into one great national unit, arousing and exalting the group instincts of nationalism, to a point that has made it possible for the Soviet government to ask their people for any sacrifice to defend and strengthen the Soviet state.

The nationalist passions of all the heterogeneous peoples forming the Soviet Union were aroused and inflamed by the same oratory, the same slogans, the same flags, music, uniforms, as in capitalist countries. To build up the power of the nation-state, the people had to give up all hope of a better material life for a long time to come. The production of consumer goods was kept to a minimum to concentrate the entire productive power of the nation on the manufacture of war material and reserves.

It is useless to express opinions on the righteousness or unrighteousness of this turn. It is a historical fact. June, 1941, proved how necessary it was. Stalingrad proved how successful.

This change of course in economic policy created much dissent among the peasant and working masses. But this smoldering opposition was ruthlessly extinguished by the central administration which, under growing internal opposition on one side and the growing external pressure created by the deteriorating international situation on the other, became every day more dictatorial, more tyrannical. The aspirations of the Russian people to a greater degree of individual freedom and political democracy, so manifest during the first decade of the Soviet Union, were slowly strangled, and in the late 1930's it was clear that from a political point of view the Soviet state was developing not toward democracy but toward absolute state control, toward complete and totalitarian domination of society by an autocratic state administration.

Communist economy is based on two completely unreal and fictitious conceptions.

The first is the overemphasized importance attached to "ownership" of tools and means of production. The development of industrialism in capitalist countries clearly shows that, as mass production becomes more complex, ownership of tools and means of production becomes more diffused and anonymous, is more widely scattered among thousands and hundreds of thousands of shareholders who have practically no control over the actual handling of their property. When a private enterprise is owned by a great number of people, it is managed more or less as a socialist or state-owned enterprise. As regards actual management and the relationship between owners and employees, there is no difference whatever between the American or British railroad companies owned by private capital, and the Scandinavian, German, Italian or Soviet railroads, owned by the state. The employees of the Bell Telephone Company, a private enterprise in America, stand in exactly the same position toward the ownership of the invested capital as do the employees of the British, French and Soviet telephone companies, owned by the state.

Twenty-five years of "Communist" regime in Russia have conclusively demonstrated that recognition of private property is almost indispensable to a smoothly working economic system. A man with initiative and imagination, or one who works hard and is thrifty, is bound to possess more wealth and achieve a higher position than the average worker who merely carries out orders, who has no personal initiative, who works no more than he can help and who spends everything he earns. After twenty-five years of "Communist" economy, the range of incomes in Soviet Russia is just as great, if not greater, than the range of incomes in capitalist countries. With this similarity, almost identity, of actual conditions and developments between the Soviet Union and the countries of private enterprise, it matters little to the worker *who* "owns" the plants and machines. For all practical purposes, it is irrelevant. At the present stage of industrialism there is little or no difference in the situation of the worker employed in the Magnitogorsk Works owned by the Soviet state, or the worker employed by private enterprises like Imperial Chemicals or General Motors.

There is no reason why creative minds like Edison, Ford, Citroen or Siemens should be prevented from building up and "owning" great industrial properties, although it may be dangerous to the community and detrimental to society if they remain the private property of second or third generation nonconstructive heirs. But with rising inheritance taxes, this problem has virtually been solved in most countries. It is only a small step from where death duties stand in England today, for instance, to the complete abolition of the right of inheritance of capital. And this step may quite possibly be taken in a none-too-distant future. Already a great industrial enterprise created by one individual is usually transformed during his lifetime into a corporation of widespread anonymous ownership under a separate management.

The second fallacy of Communism is that the main problem of economy is distribution. The sad truth is that if today we could divide total annual world production equally among the members of the entire human race, the result would be— poverty. If we divided all incomes equally among all men, the general standard of living would scarcely be above that of a Chinese coolie. In spite of our pride in the "miraculous" industrial achievements of the United States, England, Germany and Russia, our production lags miserably behind existing scientific and technical potentialities.

That nationalism and the nation-state represent insurmountable barriers to the development of an individualist capitalist economic system—the system of free enterprise—should be apparent by now to everybody. High tariff walls, export subsidies, exchange manipulations, dumping, cartels, the artificial creation of industries through government financing, etc., have completely distorted the free play of economic forces as understood by the classical theorists of the early nineteenth century. The all-important trend of our age is to strengthen the nation-state. In the presence of constant threats emanating from other nation-states, the people of each nation have been forced to centralize more and more power in their national governments.

But the similarity, indeed, the exact identity of the development of a socialist economic system within a nation-state, with the development of the capitalist system under the same conditions, is still not fully understood. To point out a few anomalies existing between fact and theory may throw light on the subject.

According to Karl Marx, the state is the result of the breaking up of society into irreconcilable, antagonistic classes. Friedrich Engels explains in his *Origin of the Family, Private Property and the State* that the state arises when and where class antagonisms cannot be objectively reconciled. And, as Lenin put it, the existence of the state proves that class antagonisms are irreconcilable.

So, according to the Marxist theory, the state is

an organ of class domination, an organ of oppression of one class by the other; "its aim is the creation of 'order' which legalizes and perpetuates this oppression by moderating the collisions between the classes." In his *State and Revolution,* Lenin arrives at the conclusion that "the state could neither arise nor maintain itself if a reconciliation of classes were possible."

And from here, only one step is necessary to arrive at the conclusion expressed by Engels in his *AntiDühring,* that once the proletariat seizes state power and transforms the means of production into state property, "it puts an end to all class differences and class antagonisms, it puts an end also to the state as the state... As soon as there is no longer any class of society to be held in subjection; as soon as, along with class domination and the struggle for individual existence based on the former anarchy of production, the collisions and excesses arising from these have also been abolished, there is nothing more to be repressed, and a special repressive force, a state, is no longer necessary...government over persons is replaced by the administration of things and the direction of the processes of production. The state is not 'abolished,' *it withers away.*"

This theory of the state and of its "withering away" after a socialist revolution is one of the main arguments in the writings of Lenin, who regarded it as a fundamental doctrine of Communism. He develops the thesis that the bourgeois state, whether monarchic or republican, absolute or democratic, is "a special repressive force" which can be demolished only by violent revolution. But once the dictatorship of the proletariat has abolished classes, the state will "become dormant." To quote Lenin from his *State and Revolution*: "The bourgeois state can only be *put an end to* by a revolution. The state in general...can only *wither away.*" Or, otherwise expressed by Lenin: "The replacement of the bourgeois by the proletarian state is impossible without a violent revolution. The abolition of the proletarian state, i.e., of all states, is only possible through *withering away.*"

In his *Poverty of Philosophy* Marx writes that once the working class replaces the old bourgeois society "by an association which excludes classes and their antagonism...there will no longer be any real political power, for political power is precisely the official expression of the class antagonism within bourgeois society."

In criticizing previous bourgeois revolutions, in *The Eighteenth Brumaire of Louis Bonaparte,* Marx roundly criticizes the parliamentary republics for centralizing and strengthening the resources of government. "All revolutions [he writes] brought this machine to greater perfection, instead of breaking it up."

This thought is developed in the *Communist Manifesto* and Lenin gives it clear expression when he says in *State and Revolution* that: "All revolutions which have taken place up to the present have helped to perfect the state machinery,

whereas it must be shattered, broken to pieces..."
These lessons "lead us to the conclusion that the
proletariat cannot overthrow the bourgeoisie
without first conquering political power, without
obtaining political rule, without transforming the
state into the proletariat organized as the ruling
class; and that this proletarian state will begin to
wither away immediately after its victory, because
in a society without class antagonisms, the state is
unnecessary and impossible."

Before digging further into the "scientific"
conclusions and predictions of Marx, Engles and
Lenin about the nature of the state and its auto-
matic and immediate "withering away" after its
conquest by the proletariat, let us pause for a
moment to compare these prophecies with the
realities of the Soviet state, with what it has
become after a quarter of a century of existence.

Lenin said: "The centralized state power
peculiar to bourgeois society came into being in
the period of the fall of absolutism. Two institutions are especially characteristic of this state
machinery: bureaucracy and the standing army."

What would be the reactions of Lenin's comrades in the *Politburo* if he were able to make this
statement in Moscow twenty years after his death?

Thundering against "those Philistines who have
brought socialism to the unheard of disgrace of
justifying and embellishing the imperialist war by
applying to it the term of 'national defense' "—
Lenin proclaims: "Bureaucracy and the standing
army constitute a 'parasite'...a parasite born of the

internal antagonisms which tear that society asunder, but essentially a parasite 'clogging every pore' of existence."

What would be the reaction of the Soviet leaders if Lenin should arise from his mausoleum and make that speech in the Red Square today?

And what would the marshals of the Red Army and the high dignitaries of Soviet diplomacy say if, twenty years after his death, in talking about the role of state power in Communist society, Lenin were to repeat that it "can be reduced to such simple operations of registration, filing and checking that they will be quite within the reach of every literate person, and it will be possible to perform them for 'workingman's wages' which circumstance can (and must) strip those functions of every shadow of privilege, of every appearance of 'official grandeur.' "

And what would the families of Lenin's comrades of the revolutionary days of 1917 think if, remembering the events of 1936 and 1937, they reread the statement Lenin made at the time of the revolution: "We set ourselves the ultimate aim of destroying the state, i.e., every organized and systematic violence, every use of violence against man in general."

The contradictions are even more striking if we turn to the writings of the founders of Communism and their views concerning the role of law and the relationship of the individual to the state.

In *State and Revolution* Lenin wrote: "Only in Communist society when the resistance of the capitalists has been completely broken, when the capitalists have disappeared, when there are no classes...only then *the state ceases to exist* and it *becomes possible to speak of freedom*...only then will democracy itself begin to *wither away* due to the simple fact that, free from capitalist slavery, from the untold horrors, savagery, absurdities and infamies of capitalist exploitation, people will gradually *become accustomed* to the observance of the elementary rules of social life that have been known for centuries and repeated for thousands of years in all school books; they will become accustomed to observing them without force, without compulsion, without subordination, without the *special apparatus* for compulsion which is called the state."

A few more short quotations from Lenin are necessary to a comparison of socialist theory and socialist reality.

"Communism renders the state absolutely unnecessary, for there is *no one* to be suppressed—no one in the sense of a *class*, in the sense of a systematic struggle with a definite section of the population."

"While the state exists there is no freedom. When there is freedom there will be no state."

"The more complete the democracy, the nearer the moment when it begins to be unnecessary."

And to the question as to how the state, standing army, bureaucracy and compulsion will "wither away" in a Communist system through the dictatorship of the proletariat, Lenin answers with the dogmatism of a high priest: "We do not know how quickly and in what succession, but we know that they will wither away. With their withering away, the state will also wither away."

These doctrines might have been taught two thousand years ago, in some primitive rural community. But it is somewhat astonishing to hear them put forth in the second decade of the twentieth century.

The theory that the state is created by the struggle between the capitalist and proletariat classes and that, once the capitalist class is done away with, state machinery would be unnecessary and would therefore disappear, is in total contradiction to existing facts and to the teachings of history. Of course, conflict between groups within a given society necessitates the creation of law and the use of force by the community to prevent violence between the two conflicting groups. But it is difficult to understand how otherwise scientifically trained minds could make the assertion that class struggle *alone* is the source of the state and that the only purpose of the state is to perpetuate the domination of one class by another.

Law and coercion in society are necessitated by thousands and thousands of conflicts arising within a given society between individuals and groups of individuals in innumerable fields, among which, in modern times, *one* is unquestionably the class struggle.

The state is not a diabolic device invented by a ruling class to oppress another class. It is the product of historical evolution. From ancient times, when magicians and priests in primitive tribes proclaimed and enforced the first rules of human conduct, up to the establishment of British constitutional monarchy, the republican constitution of the United States, the constitution of the Soviet Union, all history of civilization passing upward through families, tribes, villages, cities, provinces, principalities, kingdoms, republics, empires, commonwealths and modern nation-states, the one fundamental and invariable motive of this evolution has been that human beings, taken individually or in any given division of groups, whether vertical or horizontal, whether racial, linguistic, religious or national, are constantly in conflict with each other and that, in order to prevent these permanent and manifold clashes of interest from degenerating into violence, certain rules are necessary, certain restrictions and limitations on human impulses must be imposed and an authority established to represent the community with the right and the power to enforce such regulations and restrictions on the members of that community.

The Ten Commandments given to Moses on Mount Sinai, the writing of the Koran by Mohammed, the commands of Darius and Genghis Khan, are identical in purpose with the laws enacted by Parliament in London, Congress in Washington and the Supreme Soviet in Moscow. The differences are only changes in form throughout one long historical evolution. All these rules and regulations of human conduct, in no matter what form laid down, were devised to enable men to live together in a given society.

Who should have decisive influence in formulating these rules, what should be their content, to whom they should apply, how and by whom they should be carried out, how should they be changed, by whom and how their creation and application controlled—these have been the eternal questions of man as a member of society and on these questions political struggles have centered for thousands of years and will center for thousands of years to come.

During the past fifty years we have been passing through a stage in this long development where modern industrialism has created a conflict between those who own or manage industrial enterprises and those who function as wage earners in that system. The conflict between the capitalist class and the proletariat is doubtless deep and acute, and a solution to this problem must be found. But to say that in our age this is the *only* conflict between groups of men and that, with the resolving of that conflict, the state as such can or will disappear since it will become "unnecessary" is an altogether fantastic and unrealistic conclusion.

In 1917, in the midst of the first World War, Lenin wrote in his preface to the first edition of *State and Revolution:* "The foremost countries are being converted—we speak here of their 'rear'—into military convict labor prisons for the workers.

How right Lenin was in pointing out that as a result of international wars, states are becoming "convict labor prisons." But how wrong he was in attributing this to class struggle.

In all the Marxist analysis of the state and of the development of the state toward more and more bureaucratic and militaristic institutions, there is not one word about the real cause of this development—nationalism. There is not one word about the fact that the nation-states are in conflict with each other, a conflict which is bound to find expression in recurrent wars. There is not one word that these wars between national units are caused, not by the internal structure of the economic and social system within these individual nation-states but by the fact that they are independent, sovereign units whose relationship is unregulated.

In saying that after establishment of the dictatorship of the proletariat and the Communist system of economy, the "state will wither away" and that in a "classless" society, coercive law and the use of force will not be necessary, because once everyone is a "worker," the people will acquire the "habit" of behaving in society so that the state machinery will not be necessary—Marx the theorist and Lenin the realist show themselves to be greater utopians than the early socialists they so mercilessly lashed with their powerful didactic minds. The belief that institutions can change human nature is indeed the dominant feature of all utopias.

Social and political institutions are the result of

human behavior, the product of man. Periodically they become obsolete and require improvement or even radical reform, not to change human nature, but to make it possible for men to live together, with their existing and unchangeable character-istics, in changed circumstances.

Lenin's assertion that freedom will exist only when the state has been abolished, is another dialectic distortion, a superficial observation and a most erroneous conclusion.

It proves that he had no understanding of the real meaning of freedom.

Far from being the result of the abolition of the state, freedom in human society is exclusively the product of the state. It is indeed unthinkable with-out the state.

There is no freedom in the jungle. Freedom does not exist among animals, except the freedom of the beast of prey, the freedom of the strong to devour the weak. Freedom as an ideal is essential-ly a human ideal. It is the exact opposite of the freedom of the tiger and the shark. Human free-dom is freedom from being killed, robbed, cheat-ed, oppressed, tortured and exploited by the stronger. It means protection of the individual against innumerable dangers.

Experience demonstrates that during all our history, there has been one method and one method alone to approach that ideal. The method is: Law.

Human freedom is *created* by law and can exist only within a legal order, never without or beyond it. Naturally, through changing conditions and economic and technical developments, new situations constantly arise in which certain individuals or groups of individuals find that their freedom is menaced by newly arisen circumstances or insufficiently protected by existing laws. In all such cases, the law must be revised and amended. New restrictions, new laws create additional freedoms.

The required new freedom, made necessary by new conditions, results from the promulgation of new laws, by the granting of new, additional protection to the individuals by the community. Freedom is in no way created by the abolition of the source of such protection.

Twenty-five years after the creation of the first Communist state based on the principles of Marx, Engles and Lenin, the Soviet Union has developed into the greatest nation-state on earth, with an all-powerful bureaucracy, the largest standing army in the world, a unique police force controlling and supervising the activities of every Soviet citizen, a new social hierarchy with exceptional rewards and privileges for those in leading positions in the state, the army, the party or industry, with incomes a hundred times or more higher for the privileged few than for the average wage earner.

The Soviet people may say that it is unjust to blame the Communist regime for having developed into a strong, centralized state with a powerful army and bureaucracy. They may say that this was necessary, because the Soviet Union was surrounded by hostile capitalist states which forced them to change their original program and policy for more democracy and higher standards of living, into a policy of armaments and preparedness for national defense.

Precisely.

But in this inevitable process, the fact that the U.S.S.R. was Communist and the other countries were capitalist is totally irrelevant. England and Germany were both capitalist when they went to war. Nor was the United States Communist when it was attacked by Japan.

The one major cause of the development of the Soviet Union into a powerful centralized state and not into a "withering away" of that state, is that there were *other* sovereign power units in existence outside the U.S.S.R. and that as long as there are several sovereign power units, several national sovereignties, they are bound to conflict, no matter what their internal economic or social systems. And irrespective of their internal economic and social systems, these units, under the threat of conflict, are irresistibly driven to strengthen their own national power.

It would have been extremely interesting to watch Communist society develop in Soviet Russia without any outside pressure, in a complete absence of interference and disturbance from outside forces. But on this earth it is impossible to create laboratory conditions for social experiments. The world as it is, is the only place where social experiments can be carried out.

To state that Russia's tremendous development

in the first twenty-five years of the Soviet regime has virtually nothing to do with socialism and Communism is not to be interpreted as disparaging the positive achievements of the Soviet government and the Russian people during this quarter century. The strides made in industrialization, production, education, organization, science and the arts, have been fabulous indeed. But in this respect, Russia has done nothing unique. The very same progress had already been achieved in many capitalist countries and with democratic political institutions.

What the Soviet regime has demonstrated is the important fact that in spite of skepticism and hostility in capitalist countries, a Communist economy *can* create heavy industry, build huge mechanized factories, produce armaments and organize a powerful centralized state just as well as any capitalist country.

The rapid adaptation of the Soviet Union to the existing world order is a most striking phenomenon.

During the second World War, at all international meetings called to discuss the shape of a new world organization, the representatives of the Soviet Union have been defending exactly the same position—that of unrestricted national sovereignty—as did Lodge, Johnson and Borah in the United States Senate at the end of the first World War. The most stubborn of American isolationist Senators of 1919 would undoubtedly agree heartily with the views advocated a quarter century later by the country which claims to be and is regarded as the most revolutionary and "international" of all the countries.

Soviet foreign policy developed along exactly the same lines as that of any other major power—a policy of alliances and spheres of influence, resorting to expediency and compromise in weak situations, unilateral decisions and expansion after military victories. The Soviet Union even puts its diplomats into uniform with no stint of gold lace. In the third decade of its existence, the Soviet government is clearly pursuing power politics, the same power politics as czarist Russia or any other great country pursued when able to do so, no matter what its internal regime. They are playing the game even better. As a result of the profound upheaval in the Russian social structure and restratification that follows every revolution, a great number of first-class talents in every field emerged from Russia's immense human reservoir. The nationalist Soviet statesmen, diplomats and generals are patently more talented than the statesmen, diplomats and generals in other countries engaged in the international struggle for national supremacy. It is apparent that the political and military leadership of the U.S.S.R. is much more astute, shrewd and cunning—and consequently more successful—than that of the older democratic countries where military and political preferment are not easily obtainable by merit alone.

However, all these assets held by Soviet Russia have nothing to do with socialism or Communism.

They are the achievements of a first generation of vigorous, self-made men and the results of a national revolution. The same upsurge took place after radical changes in the history of the United States, France, England and many other countries.

Some people are convinced that nationalism in Soviet Russia—which has been in the ascendant since the death of Lenin and has become so manifest during the second World War—is nothing but a means, a new technique of Stalin to spread Communism and to bring to pass Lenin's original dream: world revolution. History will most probably be of just the opposite opinion. Long before the first centenary of the Soviet Union, it will be apparent that Communism was but a means to the end, to the great end of nationalism.

The tremendous achievement of the first twenty-five years of the Soviet regime was the creation of a centralized, powerful nationalist state.

Under Lenin and for several years after his death, the Soviet regime was not at all what it is today.

There was a great deal of individual freedom, there were open and public discussions, criticism of the government and of the party in the press and on the platforms. Not until later did the system develop into a totalitarian state with an all-powerful police force, the suppression of free speech, free criticism and all individual liberty. The development of the Soviet Union into a totalitarian dictatorship has run parallel with the awakening and growth of nationalism and the strengthening of the nation-state.

The first few years of the Soviet regime proved that socialism is not incompatible with political freedoms. It was the influence and pressure of nationalism that forced the regime to evolve into a totalitarian dictatorship. And in traveling the road toward the totalitarian state, the Soviet regime destroyed not only political freedom but also the principles of socialist society as they were understood and proclaimed by Lenin and his associates in 1917.

Since the 1920's, Communism has been diminishing in importance and nationalism has been growing by leaps and bounds. During these first twenty-five years, the Communist Internationale, in spite of innumerable attempts, failed to spread the influence of Moscow abroad. But the totalitarian Soviet nation-state succeeded. Even the many Communist parties in foreign countries, unquestionably inspired by Moscow, have given up their fight for the socialization of their countries and become merely the instruments of Soviet Russia's nationalist policy, adopting in each country an attitude dictated not by the necessity of fostering Communism, but by the necessity of strengthening the international position of the Soviet Union as a nation-state.

In the second World War, the Communists in every country have become more nationalist than any monarchists, landowners or industrialists anywhere. They have provided the vanguard of "patriotic" forces in every country.

The passionate debates, the international strife existing between the protagonists of capitalism and socialism, seem of secondary importance if we take into consideration the following undeniable facts:

a. A state-controlled economy can build factories and produce commodities just as well as a system of free enterprise.

b. Ownership of capital, tools and means of production does not appreciably affect either the economic or the social structure of a state.

c. Under both capitalism and socialism ownership tends to become impersonal.

d. In both systems, employed, salaried management is the real master of the economic machinery.

e. Socialism *per se* does not raise the material standard of the workers nor does it secure for them a higher degree of political and economic freedom.

f. Economic and political security and freedom depend upon specific social legislation which can be and in varied degrees has been evolved both in capitalist and in socialist countries.

g. Socialism cannot prevent international conflicts any more than can capitalism.

h. Under the present political structure of the world, both capitalism and socialism are dominated by nationalism and actively support the institution of the nation-state.

i. The permanent state of distrust and fear

between nation-states and the recurring armed conflicts between them have the same effects on capitalist and on socialist economy, neither being able to develop under the constant threat of war.

In view of these facts, there seems to be no place for dogmatism in connection with the dispute between capitalism and socialism. Both proclaim their aim to be an economy of rational mass production, full exploitation of modern technological and scientific methods to raise the material and cultural standards of the masses. Which system can best accomplish this task should be decided by experience, not by cracking each other's skulls in a senseless class warfare. If certain people—like the Slavs—through their century-old traditions, have an inclination toward collective ownership of farm lands, pastures or modern industrial plants and prefer a socialist system, and if other peoples —like the Latins and Anglo-Saxons—through their century-old traditions and inclinations, prefer an individualist and private ownership economy, there is not the slightest reason why these different methods should not be able to coexist and co-operate with each other. To concentrate on differences of opinion and habit, and to believe that this is the field on which will be fought the great battles of the twentieth century, is an unfortunate confusion of issues.

We can continue this class struggle for decades. It may even be that one of the two classes will defeat and dominate the other. But whether we continue this internecine strife forever or whether one system achieves victory over the other, the solution of the problem of the twentieth century will not be advanced a single step.

This analysis of trends in the Soviet Union is in no way intended to be anti-Communist or anti-Russian, just as the analyses of similar trends in the United States, Great Britain and other capitalist-democratic countries are not intended to be anti-capitalist, anti-American, anti-British or anti-anything. The conclusions are not directed against any nation, any social system, any economic order. Far from it, they seek to prove the irrelevancy and complete uselessness of class accusations and how superficial is criticism based on the belief that any economic system *as such* is capable of solving the issues with which we have to deal.

Our endeavor is to demonstrate that it is the political *status quo*—the existing system of sovereign nation-states, accepted and upheld today by capitalists and socialists, individualists and collectivists, all national and religious groups alike—that constitutes the insurmountable obstacle to all progress, to all social and economic efforts, that bars all human progress on *any* lines.

The conflict between our static, inherited political institutions and the realities of economic and social dynamism is the real issue to which we must address ourselves.

The underlying thesis of Marxist historical materialism, that history is nothing but a class struggle moved solely or preponderantly by the profit motive, the economic self-interest of the dominating classes, is an oversimplification which pays undue tribute to human intelligence and reason.

It would be extremely easy to solve social problems if the motor of human action were such a clearly definable, materialist driving force. The trouble is that man is not such a reasonable creature. History is molded by much more volcanic, much more primitive forces, much more difficult to control and to deal with than the economic self-interest of individuals or classes. The real powers of historical evolution have always been and are today more than ever, transcendental emotions, tribal instincts, beliefs, faith, fear, hatred and superstition.

And Marxism, in spite of its scientific aspirations, has merely created another set of emotional fears, superstitions and taboos which have become a very strong force in the present world convulsion, but which is only one of many such emotional forces at work today.

It might advance a dispassionate approach to the sterile and now century-old controversy, if the champions of capitalism and socialism would realize that they are fighting each other within a hermetically sealed conveyance. The fight for a better seat, for a broader view, for a little more comfort is rather meaningless, as they are being carried by it relentlessly toward the same terminus. The vehicle is nationalism. The terminus is totalitarianism.

CHAPTER IV

FAILURE OF RELIGION

THE wholesale murder, torture, persecution and oppression we are witnessing in the middle of the twentieth century proves the complete bankruptcy of Christianity as a civilizing force, its failure as an instrument to tame instinctive human passions and to transform man from an animal into a rational social being.

The revival of barbarism and the wholesale practice of mass murder all over the world cannot be regarded as the work of a few godless, sadistic Gestapo men and some fanatic believers in Shintoism. It is being practiced by many churchgoing men of many nationalities.

Millions of innocent people have been murdered in cold blood, tens of millions have been robbed, deported and enslaved by Christians, descendants of families belonging for centuries to the Roman Catholic, Greek Catholic and Protestant churches. Cruelties, horrible and inhuman beyond imagination, have been committed by countless men, not only German and Japanese, but Spanish, Italian, Polish, Rumanian, Hungarian, French, Serbian, Croatian and Russian. And these deeds, surpassing in ferocity and bloodthirstiness anything hitherto recorded in Western history, have been tolerated, and therefore tacitly admitted, by each and every organized Christian religion.

There is no intention here to accuse or to pass judgment upon any of the organized religions for tolerating these outbreaks of prehistoric, atavistic animalism in man. But the very fact that such a radical reversion has occurred proves the utter inadequacy of the methods followed by the Christian religions to influence and mold human character and to make man follow, not his own brutal instincts but something in the nature of moral principles.

It cannot be denied that Christianity has failed to penetrate the soul of man, to take root in human character. It has succeeded only in creating a fragile veneer of ethical conduct, a thin crust of civilization which has been blasted away and blown to pieces by the volcanic social eruptions of the twentieth century.

For a certain time there was some justification for the belief that the Judaeo-Christian principles were triumphing through their effective ritualism and the mystical presentation of their dogmas, which filled simple, primitive men with enough awe and fear to induce them to follow the teachings of Christianity, not because they understood them and wanted them but because they feared the Uncertain and the Unknown. But today, since modern science has destroyed or made ridiculous most of the age-old superstitions and venerated symbols—the necessary and useful media for the propagation of ideals centuries ago—the ideals alone are powerless to direct and regulate human conduct in society.

We have to recognize that the Ten Commandments, the moral teachings of the prophets, of Christ, the evangelists and the Apostles, cannot be made a reality in this world of enlightenment, science, technical progress and communications by using methods devised centuries ago by the founders of religions, according to the circumstances of their time—methods which are wholly ineffective today. It in no way derogates from the great work and the good intentions of the religions, nor is it anything to be ashamed of if we realize and admit that man, to be transformed from the beast he is to a responsible member of a civilized society, needs methods more effective than prayer, sermons and ritual.

Man can become a conscious and constructive social being only if society imposes upon him certain principles in the form of a legal order.

History demonstrates indisputably that there is only one method to make man accept moral principles and standards of social conduct. That method is: Law.

Peace among men and a civilized society—which are one and the same thing—are imaginable only within a legal order equipped with institutions to give effect to principles and norms in the form of law, with adequate power to apply those laws and to enforce them with equal vigor against all who violate them.

This self-evident truth—supported by the entire history of mankind—can hardly be the subject of debate any longer.

Just as prayer, sermons and ritual are inadequate to impose upon mankind a social conduct based on principles, so pledges, declarations and promises are inadequate to achieve the same purpose.

Throughout the entire history of all known civilizations, only one method has ever succeeded in creating a social order within which man had security from murder, larceny, cheating and other crimes, and had freedom to think, to speak and to worship.

That method is Law.

And integrated social relations regulated by law—which is peace—have been possible only within social units of indivisible sovereignty, with one single source of law, irrespective of the size, territory, population, race, religion and degree of complexity of such social units. It has *never* been possible *between* such sovereign social units, even if they were composed of populations of the same race, the same religion, the same language, the same culture, the same degree of civilization.

The failure of Christianity as a civilizing force of society is an incalculable tragedy.

Two thousand years is time enough to judge the efficacy of a method, no matter how valuable the doctrine. During these twenty centuries, it has seemed at times that Christianity had at last succeeded in taming the beast in man, in controlling and directing destructive human impulses and characteristics.

But since the Christian churches have deviated from their universal mission and have evolved into national organizations supporting the pagan, tribal instincts of nationalism everywhere, we see how weak was the hold of Christianity upon the Western world. For worldly interests they have abandoned their moral teachings and have capitulated before the volcanic instincts of man, who are bound to destroy each other, unless restricted by universal law.

What was divine and civilizing in Christianity was its monotheism, its universalism. The doctrine which teaches that all men are created equal in the sight of God and are ruled by one God, with one law over all men, was the one really revolutionary idea in human history.

Unfortunately, organized Christianity developed into a more and more dogmatic, totalitarian hierarchy and the reaction to it led first to schism, then to widespread sectarianism. Thus the ideal of universal law has degenerated on one side into more and more centralized absolutism, and on the other into more and more widely separated sects and denominations. At the moment modern nations began to crystallize and national feeling in the Western world began to prevail over Christian feeling, the Christian churches, already divided among themselves, split into a number of new sects, each supporting the rising ideal of the nation.

Nationalism soon became identified with Christianity and in every country nationalist policy was recognized as Christian policy, in opposition to liberal and socialist tendencies.

Since the abandonment of universalism by the Christian churches—Catholic as well as Protestant—they have diverged from the original fundamental doctrine of Christianity to which they adhere no longer except in name. In thousands of churches today, Catholic priests and Protestant preachers of all denominations are praying for the glory of their own nationals and for the downfall of others, even if they belong to the same church. This is indeed in violent contradiction to the highest religious ideal mankind ever produced—universal Christianity.

A universal moral principle is neither universal nor moral, nor is it a principle if it is valid only within segregated groups of people. "Thou shalt not kill" cannot mean that it is a crime to kill a man of one's own nationality, but that it is a virtue—to be blessed by all Christian churches—to kill a man of the same faith, who happens to be technically the citizen or subject of another nation-state. Such an interpretation of universal moral principles is revolting.

The same development can be observed in the second great monotheistic creed, in Islam. The great unity which had been maintained by the Koran for so many centuries among peoples of different stock, from the Atlas to the Himalaya Mountains, has been visibly splitting up into nationalist groups within which allegiance to the new nationalist ideal is more powerful than loyalty to the old universal teachings of Mohammed.

There is Pan-Turkism or Pan-Turanism, aimed at the union of all branches of the Turkish race living in the region extending from the Dardanelles to the Tigris and Euphrates.

To the south, the rising Pan-Arab movement is advocating the federation of all the Arab tribes into one nation.

Farther to the east—in India—the believers in Islam are inflamed by a strong Indian national feeling, expressed in the slogan: "I am an Indian first, a Muslim afterwards."

And among the Mohammedan populations of the Soviet Union there burns a passionate Soviet nationalism.

Not only Christianity and Islam with their vast numbers of believers are being completely absorbed and dominated by neopagan nationalism. Even the originators of monotheism, even the Jews, have forgotten the fundamental teaching of their religion: universalism.

They seem no longer to remember that the One and Almighty God first revealed Himself to them because He chose them for a special mission, to spread the doctrine of the oneness of the Supreme Lawgiver, the universal validity of monotheism among the people of the world. They too, just like the followers of other monotheistic creeds, have become abject idolaters of the new polytheism—nationalism.

With glowing passion they desire nothing more than to worship their own national idol, to have their own nation-state. No amount of persecution and suffering can justify such abandonment of a world mission, such total desertion of universalism for nationalism, another name for the very tribalism which is the origin of all their misfortunes and miseries.

It is of utmost importance for the future of mankind to realize the apostasy and failure of all three of the monotheistic world religions and their domination by disruptive and destructive nationalism, as without the deep influence of the monotheistic outlook of Judaism, Christianity and Islam, human freedom in society—democracy—could never have been instituted and cannot survive.

Democracy, political freedom, the political rights of the individual, the equality of man before the law—all the things we have in mind when talking about democracy—are the products of Greek philosophy and Judaeo-Christian ethics. Democracy and political independence as we conceive them today are essentially the fruits of Western civilization. The roots of democratic ideals, of course, are much deeper. Village communities in India were run on a democratic basis centuries before the Greek cities. Meng-tse in China expressed views similar to Jefferson's long before the Christian Era. But the organization of powerful nations in centralized democratic states is something entirely new in human history, and it is the product of universal monotheism. For Aristotle a democratic state was not conceivable with more than ten thousand inhabitants. Fifteen centuries of

Judaeo-Christian-Islamic teaching about man created in the image of God, about the equality of man before God, were needed to forge the ideology of modern political democracy.

The free thinkers of the eighteenth century, who were among the pioneers of modern political democracy, revolted, not against the moral teaching of monotheism, but against the immoral practices and superstitions of the churches as national, human institutions. In fact, those free thinkers, in spite of the anathema cast upon them by the organized churches, were the most faithful disciples of the monotheistic conception since the prophets of Israel and the Apostles of Christ.

There have been and there are other civilizations.

Among them the two most important are the Chinese and the Indian. But those great Asiatic civilizations are based on religious ideals, on notions of the relationship of man to man and man to God, entirely different from ours. Neither the Chinese nor the Indian peoples have ever had, nor have they ever yearned for the political and social system we in the Occident call democracy.

To us, there is something wrong and unjust about inequality and poverty. Our political struggles and aspirations tend to limit, if not abolish, social injustice, to create more goods and a more equitable distribution of wealth. Having made men more or less equal before the law and given them equal political rights, we seek to equalize their material conditions also. At least, that is the motivating ideal, however far we may be from achieving it.

In India, China, Japan—throughout the Orient where more than half the human race lives—inequalities are not regarded as a social injustice. Indeed, their whole system of religious thought is a direct justification of poverty, social inequality and the caste system.

How could democracy exist among the believers in Shintoism, which teaches that the earthly rulers themselves are gods? A creed having countless gods, in which every household deifies its ancestors, in which the greater gods preside over the empire and the lesser gods over towns and hamlets and which teaches that the emperor, an absolute monarch, is a god himself and the direct descendant of the sun-goddess, obviously precludes any reforms in the inherited structure of that society.

In even more striking contrast to democratic society are the great Asiatic religions, Brahmanism, Buddhism, Hinduism. These creeds, in which hundreds of millions of people dogmatically believe, are simultaneously religious and social institutions. Their two basic doctrines are:

1. A polytheistic pantheism, with an endless number of gods.
2. Metempsychosis, the transmigration of souls or reincarnation.

The entire social fabric of six to eight hundred million people is woven from these doctrines which dominate the everyday life and validate the morality of nearly half the human race. For them only one reality exists—Brahma—an absolute, all embracing spirit, the original cause and ultimate goal of all individual souls. This faith teaches that the soul is immortal, that each soul goes through endless reincarnations, and that no one can change, or has even the right to seek a change in his present condition of existence. Any desire for betterment in earthly conditions is a sin. Only through piety can a man strive to improve his lot, not in the present life but in future incarnations. The unbelievable poverty, abject misery and sub-animal existence of the sixty million untouchables in India, for instance, cannot be altered, since they are believed to be suffering in this life the just punishment for sins committed in previous incarnations.

Such a creed naturally goes hand in hand with gross superstitions, the worship of hosts of godlings, ghosts, spirits, demons and mystic objects of every kind. Approximately four-fifths of the people of southern India, while commonly acknowledging the spiritual guidance of the Brahmans, worship local village deities with animal sacrifices and primitive rites.

The entire social structure reflects these religious ideas. One of the cardinal principles of society is racialism, the preservation and purity of descent. It is an aristocratic, not an egalitarian society. According to the prevailing religious principles, the society recognizes, utilizes and explains the inequalities of individuals and groups of individuals without making any attempt to remedy them.

It would be an affront to the great Asiatic peoples to criticize their traditions and their faith. Nothing is more remote from our intentions. But an analysis of the relationship between religious doctrines and principles of society demonstrates that the form of society at which the Western world is aiming is closely connected with the basic teachings of monotheism. Without its influence, modern democracy is unthinkable.

It is therefore of vital importance, from the point of view of the future of democratic institutions, human liberty and further progress of Western civilization, that the monotheistic religions recognize the incompatibility of nationalism with their basic doctrine, and the mortal danger presented to our immediate future by national disintegration and national sectarianism in the Jewish, Catholic, Protestant, Greek Orthodox and Islamic religions.

Today, nearly two centuries after Thomas Paine wrote *The Age of Reason,* his utterance is more to the point than ever: "I do not believe in the creed professed by the Jewish church, by the Roman church, by the Turkish church, by the Protestant church, nor by any church that I know of. My own mind is my own church. All national institutions of churches, whether Jewish, Christian or Turkish, appear to me no other than human inventions, set up to terrify and enslave mankind, and monopolize power and profit."

Human society can be saved only by universalism. Unless the Christian churches return to this central doctrine of their religion and make it the central doctrine of their practice, they will vanish before the irresistible power of a new religion of universalism, which is bound to arise from the ruin and suffering caused by the impending collapse of the era of nationalism.

CHAPTER V

ROAD TO FASCISM

FREE enterprise, individualist and capitalist, was wrecked on the rock of nationalism. In the abstract, its principles, as propounded by Adam Smith, David Ricardo and John Stuart Mill, are as correct today as they were at the beginning of industrialism. We see now that such a system of absolute economic freedom never existed—nor could ever exist—except within relatively wide national boundaries, at an early stage of industrial expansion and then only for a short time. It was tried in England at the beginning of the nineteenth century, but its free development was soon obstructed by the United States, Germany and other countries whose nationalism induced them to establish tariff barriers to create a national industry for their home markets and to enable themselves to compete with British industry on the world market.

From the very moment the first tariff barriers were imposed on industrial products, we could no longer speak of a system of free enterprise and free economy. Since that time, now more than a century ago, economic principles and economic necessities have been clashing with our political beliefs and fighting a losing battle. No matter how rational were the classic arguments of liberal eco-nomists, their doctrines were powerless in the face of irrational and transcendental nationalist pas-sions. To national governments—and to the great majority of the peoples—it seemed more impor-tant to build up and maintain national industries, no matter how uneconomically they functioned, than to allow their people access to the best and cheapest commodities on the market.

For a certain time tariff barriers did help certain nations to increase their wealth and raise their living standards. Large national compartments, the United States, the British Empire, even the French and German Empires, progressed rapidly and na-tionalist advocates of tariff barriers were perfectly justified in pointing out that this progress was the result of the protective walls erected around their nation-states.

Within a few decades a point was reached at which there was hardly a country whose economy could develop further based entirely on national territories and populations. The greatest industrial powers lacked raw materials, which they were forced to purchase abroad, and were unable to consume their entire production at home. Once this saturation point in the internal development of national economies was reached and interchange with the economies of other closed national systems became inevitable, the ensuing conflict between political and economic interests threw the entire economy of the world out of gear.

Unemployment surged up and the nation-states, after having intervened in the free movement of goods and services, were now forced to interfere with the free movement of peoples, with migration. This solved no problem at all. The social schism resulting from the so-called system of free enterprise—which nation-states never allowed to be free—began to dominate the political scene and socialism was born.

Although Marx and Engels made the socialist parties international, strangely enough, "nationalization," and not "internationalization" of the means of production was pursued. Obviously, the "internationalism" of the Socialist Internationale was only a tactical move, a mere label. The actual programs of the socialist parties have always been national. They advocated national solutions of the economic problem through transfer of ownership from private individuals to the nation-states.

The evolution of Western civilization in the past hundred years is best characterized by this struggle between the liberal and conservative elements upholding the ideals of free enterprise and private ownership of tools and means of production, and the socialist and Communist elements working toward state ownership of instruments of production.

Today it is clear to all—the First, Second and Third Internationales notwithstanding—that the outlook of both groups has always been and still is national. Both believe solutions of the economic and social problems to be possible and desirable on a national basis within the framework of the present nation-state structure as established in the eighteenth century, before the birth of industrialism.

Today we can survey with some degree of historical perspective the growth of both systems: the individualist system of free enterprise in Western states and the socialist-Communist system of collectivism in the Soviet Union. In both, such observation reveals the same trend toward ever-increasing nationalist state machinery and ever-growing pressure on the individual by control, regulation and infringement of his personal liberty.

In all capitalist countries the conflict between industrialism and nationalism led to higher and higher tariffs, to more and more government control of production and distribution by means of export and import regulations, quotas, taxation, supervision, direct control and active direction. Growing tension resulting from demographic pressure and economic necessity led more and more of the industrial countries to embark upon a policy of expansion, first by the conquest of foreign markets through dumping and other artificial export subventions, then by open military aggression.

The incredibly rapid development of world communications brought all the industrial powers in contact with each other, making conflicts insoluble and wars inevitable. This constant danger of attack from outside forces tremendously accelerated the already existing tendency to concentrate more and more power in the hands of centralized national governments.

Within the nation-states the conflict between eighteenth century doctrines of political democracy and early nineteenth century doctrines of free economic enterprise became even more acute after the first World War, which left all the underlying problems unsolved. In some countries where the pressure was greatest, it led to open repudiation of democratic and liberal political principles and to the establishment of a new creed, which made of necessity a virtue and proclaimed the state as the highest ultimate goal of human society, in absolute denial of the eighteenth century democratic conceptions.

The fact that the conclusions of abstract reasoning and the results of empirical observation coincide is of great help in the correct diagnosis and interpretation of the present world crisis, its causes and its symptoms.

We have seen the irresistible sequence of events which, during the past decades, has led all industrial countries, both capitalist and Communist, toward the all-powerful nation-state, in almost total contradiction to their proclaimed principles.

Developments during the first part of the twentieth century demonstrate conclusively the fallacy of the Marxist belief that capitalism is bound automatically to be transformed into Communism, that Communism is the natural product and the final result of capitalism.

During the critical twenty-five years between 1917 and 1942, not one single democratic capitalist country has become Communist nor has one adopted government ownership of all means of production. Not one single event has occurred to prove this Marxist doctrine, despite the tremendous efforts of Communist parties all over the world to conquer power and despite the deadly fears of the capitalists that they would do so.

Only in Russia has the Communist system been established, by means of revolution. Now Russia had never been a capitalist, democratic society. It had always been feudal, agricultural, illiterate, a backward conglomeration of peoples ruled by an autocratic dynasty. From the very moment of the Communist revolution—which was in complete opposition to the scientific previsions of Marx, who said Communism would grow out of capitalism and be established first in the most highly industrialized countries—from that very moment the same phenomena occurred as in capitalist countries, the same development, the same transformation, the same irresistible drive toward centralized bureaucratic state administration.

During those very same twenty-five years, however, about two dozen capitalist, democratic countries became—Fascist.

Empirical observation would indicate that the "natural product" of capitalism is not Communism but Fascism. And it seems equally clear that Communism, under certain circumstances now prevailing, moves in the same direction.

The alternative therefore appears not to be "Communism or Fascism," as was popularly believed between 1920 and 1940. Historical events during those twenty years and political facts irrefutably demonstrate that:

1. Not one capitalist, democratic country became Communist.
2. A number of capitalist, democratic countries evolved through parallel processes, toward Fascism.
3. The only existing Communist country was dominated by the same forces and also evolved into a totalitarian, Fascist state.

History will not describe socialism as having replaced or followed capitalism. Most certainly both will be recorded as parallel phenomena, expressions of one and the same era.

Socialism could not establish itself until capitalism had first begun closely to resemble socialism, until socialism itself had begun to look a good deal like capitalism. It was the transformation of capitalism into a system of economic planning, of cartels, trusts, tariffs, subsidies and other regulations, and of interference by the central political authority that paved the way for socialism. And it was the transformation of socialism from a rigid, egalitarian doctrine into an hierarchical conception with differentiations of functions and income that made socialism a workable reality. Today it is useless to contrast the two systems, as there are many socialist features in the most capitalist countries, just as there are many capitalist features in the most socialist country.

The only conclusion we can draw from these facts is that capitalism and socialism are parallel phenomena intimately blended everywhere; that Communism does not grow out of capitalism; that it can establish itself only by revolution; that within the existing nation-state structure both have a tendency—at the present stage of industrialism—to develop into centralized, bureaucratic and totalitarian regimes.

Simultaneously with this development, a new political philosophy and movement arose—Fascism—proclaiming as an ideal, as a positive aim of policy, the very social order toward which all countries were actually developing. This new Fascist movement, so diametrically opposed to all the fundamental principles of Christianity, socialism and democracy, spread like wildfire around the whole globe.

What is the historic meaning of Fascism?

We cannot answer this question without freeing ourselves from emotional prejudice. It makes for hopeless confusion to allow the terms applied to the major forces of our time to degenerate into fetish words with which to slur each other. We shall get nowhere by calling anyone who is not himself an enterpriser and who expresses doubts as to the wisdom of the political, economic and financial policies of the capitalist countries—a Communist; or by calling anyone who dares to remark that Soviet Russia is not quite a perfect Garden of Eden, or that Stalin and his government may not always and in all cases be a hundred per cent right—a Fascist. Emotional outbursts and name-calling cannot help in an effort to analyze and discuss the dominating currents of our time.

We must stop believing that Fascism is the political instrument of a few gangsters lusting for power.

It is also impossible to explain Fascism by social cleavage alone, by class warfare. The liberals say that Fascism is the result of socialism, that socialist doctrines regarding economic planning, public control of production, distribution, etc., lead straight to state domination, totalitarian dictatorship, Fascism.

But there must be a difference between socialism and Fascism. Otherwise Fascist governments, after assuming power, would not immediately dissolve trade unions and labor parties, destroy all the liberties of the workers and persecute all who called themselves socialists or who desire to advance the interests of the working class.

Socialists say that Fascism is an instrument of capitalism, that it is the highest form of capitalism, that its purpose is to oppress the working classes and to prevent their emancipation through labor unions and socialism.

This is an equally shallow point of view. The socialists cannot deny that of their own free will millions of factory workers supported and voted for Hitler, Mussolini and other Fascist dictators, that many trade unions and syndicates joined Fascist regimes and that many socialist leaders became members of Fascist governments. In face of Fascism the cleavage in proletariat ranks is just as wide as in any other section of society.

Certainly elements of both capitalism and socialism are to be found in Fascism. But its historical and sociological meaning are altogether different and much more significant.

If we try to determine the meaning of democracy, socialism and Fascism, it becomes apparent that under the pressure resulting from the nation-state structure of the world and because of the ravaging wars inherent in this structure, both the democracies and the Soviet Union are bound to evolve toward Fascism.

Among the three great powers opposing the Fascist camp in this second World War, the Soviet Union, of course, most closely approaches the ideal of totalitarianism, the ideal of a Fascist state, although Soviet citizens would vigorously deny such an allegation. But this confusion of terms is merely the result of a lack of definition. It is a game of words. There is a story about Huey Long which, whether true or not, is extremely symptomatic of our age. When the Louisiana demagogue was asked whether he believed that the United States would become Fascist, he answered: "Surely. But we shall call it anti-Fascism."

In spite of the innumerable speeches and treatises attempting to define the phenomenon of Fascism—more exactly totalitarianism—it is, even after it has conquered half the world, a nebulous notion, a rather mystical conception. The best definition of Fascism is still the article *"Fascismo"* written by Benito Mussolini in the *Enciclopedia Italiana.*

The ideology and the doctrinal foundation of Fascism are admittedly a reaction to developments of the past two centuries. According to Mussolini: "Fascism is a spiritual conception, born of the general reaction of this century against the sluggish and materialist positivism of the eighteenth century."

It is also a reaction to the age of reason in the political field. "Fascism is a religious conception in which man appears in his inherent relationship to a superior law, to an objective Will, which transcends the particular individual and elevates him as a conscious member of a spiritual society."

To induce man—confused and disillusioned by the insecurity resulting from the bankruptcy of democratic individualism in an age of conflicting nation-states—to renounce his individuality and accept complete subordination to the state in exchange for security, Mussolini surrounded the

Fascist idea with a great deal of mysticism and sophism.

"The world in the sense of Fascism is not the materialistic world it superficially appears to be, in which man is an individual distinct from all the others, standing alone, governed by a law of nature which instinctively makes him live a life of egoistic and momentary self-satisfaction. The man of Fascism is an individual who is the expression of nation and country, the expression of the moral law that binds together the people and generations in one tradition and in one mission, which does away with the instinct of a narrow life of short-lived pleasure, to establish a sense of duty toward a superior life, free from the limits of time and space: a life in which the individual, through self-abnegation, through sacrifice of his own particular interests, even through death, realizes all that spiritual existence in which lies his value as a man."

And to justify complete political and economic enslavement of the individual, he proclaims: "The individual in the Fascist State is not nullified, rather he is multiplied, just as in a regiment one soldier is not diminished but multiplied by the number of his comrades...Outside history, man is non-existent. For that reason, fascism is against all the individualist abstractions based on eighteenth century materialism; it is also against all Utopias and Jacobin innovations. Fascism does not believe in the possibility of 'happiness' on earth, as was the desire expressed in the economic literature of the 1700's..."

But underlying all this dialectic and emotional justification, Fascism has one single purpose, one single thesis, one single philosophy, which is mirrored throughout Mussolini's long exposé defining the doctrine of Fascism.

"Liberalism denied the state in the interest of the individual; Fascism reaffirms the state as the true embodiment of the individual..."

"Anti-individualist, the Fascist conception is for the state. It is for the individual only insofar as he coincides with the state, that is with the consciousness and universal will of man in his historical existence..."

There can be..."no individuals outside the state, nor any groups (political parties, associations, trade unions, classes)..."

"For the Fascist, everything is in the state, nothing human or spiritual exists, and even less anything of value exists outside the state. In this sense, Fascism is totalitarian, and the Fascist state, the synthesis and unity of all values, interprets, develops and lends potency to the whole life of the people..."

"It is not the nation which creates the state...On the contrary, the nation is created by the state, which gives the people, conscious of their own moral unity, a will, and therefore a real existence..."

"For Fascism the state is an absolute, before which individuals and groups are relative. Individuals and groups are 'thinkable' only insofar as they are within the state..."

"The state, in fact, as the universal ethical will is the creator of right..."

These categoric declarations make it clear that Fascism is not an economic conception. It is essentially a politico-social doctrine. Its aim is the absolute, untrammeled, totalitarian domination of the nation-state with complete regulation of individual life, the reduction of the individual to serfdom.

But this totalitarian, Fascist state can operate in principle just as well in capitalist economy, with private enterprise and private ownership of capital, as it can function in a socialist system of economy with centralized state planning and state ownership of capital.

Fascism is not a reaction to capitalism nor is it a reaction to socialism.

It is a reaction to democratic individualism, in no matter what economic form, under certain specific political conditions.

Totalitarian Fascism clearly represents a suppression of the social and economic conflict within the nation-states by bestowing absolute supremacy on the nation-state—the real cause of the crisis—to the detriment of free industrial development—which alone could remedy it.

The strait-jacket of nationalism and the nation-state tends to paralyze political liberty and economic freedom. In the gradual disintegration we have witnessed during the first half of the twentieth century, within one nation-state after the other, a stage was reached in which it appeared imperative for survival of the state to throw overboard the already challenged and distrusted ideals of individualism and democracy, and to establish a clear-cut dictatorship, on the pretext that complete state domination was the only solution to internal chaos and political fratricide.

The real conflict of our age is not between individualism and collectivism, nor between capitalism and Communism, but between industrialism and nationalism.

In recent history and in our own lifetime we have seen that both capitalism and socialism lead to state domination—to totalitarian Fascism. From this empirical phenomenon, we must draw the conclusions we should have reached a long time ago by rational analysis, that Fascism has nothing to do with the form of the economic system— capitalism or socialism—but with its content: industrialism.

We cannot maintain industrial progress within the nation-state structure without arriving at complete state domination and the destruction of political democracy and individual liberty—without arriving at Fascism.

To what purpose is all this mistrust, hatred and fighting between socialists and capitalists, accusing each other of totalitarianism, oppression and exploitation?

The truth is that both are becoming Fascist and totalitarian. It is high time to realize this and to start the common fight for human liberty and welfare, against the common and real enemy—the nation-state.

Both camps are more or less hypnotized by the Fascist reasoning that there can be no individual freedom without "freedom" of the state. Consequently, since the democratic machinery created to express the sovereignty of the people gets out of control as a result of internal crises within the nation-states and government becomes unstable, the view is advanced that the sovereignty of the people is best expressed by the totalitarian state. Indeed, according to Fascist theory, the power of the state is the only criterion of 'national sovereignty. In this conception, the needs of modern industrialism are completely subjugated to the dictates of an all-powerful nationalism.

Many people have thought, and still believe, that Fascism is the antithesis of or a reaction to Communism. Many democracies on their road to dictatorship have passionately debated whether they were heading toward Communism or Fascism.

People in democracies, who are trying to make up their minds whether the danger lies in Communism or in Fascism are dreaming of a freedom of decision they do not possess. There is no choice. We are moving straight toward Fascism. To a large extent, we are already there. Even should a Communist revolution succeed in one country or another, it would change nothing in our progress toward totalitarianism. The Communist countries, should there be more of them, would soon join the throng led by the irresistible Pied Piper: the sovereign nation-state.

Prevailing theories about the antagonism of Communism and Fascism are utterly fallacious.

As fallacious is the point of view that Fascism is the antithesis of or reaction to democratic capitalism.

The truth is that neither individualist capitalism nor collective socialism can work within the nation-state structure. Both are marching straight toward totalitarian Fascism. Both are creating Fascism under certain specific conditions, conditions which are activated by nationalism and the nation-state.

If we limit ourselves to a choice between national capitalism, national socialism or national Communism, it matters little which we choose. If it is to be "national" it will in any case be totalitarian Fascism.

In the last analysis, modern Fascism would seem therefore, to be the inescapable result of the conflict between industrialism and nationalism at their saturation point within the framework of a sovereign nation-state, irrespective of whether the economic system is capitalist or socialist.

PART TWO

CHAPTER VI

NATION-FEUDALISM

C ONDITIONS prevailing today in human society show striking parallels with conditions
after the reign of Charlemagne and the Carlovin-
gians, the era between the tenth and thirteenth
centuries, when the system of political feudalism
had been stabilized and was flourishing.

When the centralized rule of the known Western world collapsed with the fall of the Roman
Empire, and the Church was not sufficiently
strong and well-organized to replace the *Pax
Romana* with an equally efficient centralized
secular order, the lives and property of the people
were stripped of the necessary protection against
uprisings of the poverty-stricken, landless peasants
or against sudden attacks by invaders from the
neighboring lands.

From this chaotic stage of Western evolution
emerged feudalism, created and set into motion as
a political system by the desire of the masses for
protection and security. The landless freeman and
the small landowner went to the most powerful
lord of the land in the neighborhood and asked
for shelter and support in exchange for which
they offered their services.

The subjects submitted themselves and their

lands—if they had any—to the baron, and received from him food and shelter in peacetime and equipment in war, for which they tilled the soil, paid taxes and fought battles.

Although later the lords of the land were all vassals of the king—who became the symbol of unity—sovereign power was, for all practical purposes, vested in the individual barons. The administration of the land and of the law, of armed force and of finance were almost entirely in their hands.

Feudalism differed greatly in the various parts of Europe, but certain of its features were identical everywhere. These were:

1. The vassal-lord relationship.
2. Loyalty and mutual obligation, protection and service, binding together all the ranks of each separate feudal social unit.
3. Contractual relations of lord and tenant, determining all individual and collective rights, forming the foundation of all law.
4. Financial sovereignty of the feudal lord, with the power to tax his subjects and in some cases to coin money.
5. The juridical sovereignty of the feudal lord. His courts were the public courts, and revenue from all fines went to him.
6. The military sovereignty of the feudal lord. All subjects on the lands of the lord owed him military service, were obliged to take up arms whenever he called upon them. The feudal landlord was also the commander of the troops composed of his subjects.

7. Each feudal baron had his symbol, emblem, flag, etc., to which all subjects living on his lands owed obeisance and allegiance.

The relations between commoner and feudal landlord as demonstrated by these principles are almost the same as the relations existing today between nation-states and their citizens.

The foundation of feudal relationship was not only land. A great many other services and privileges were integrated in the system. The feudal lord conferred public offices, various sources of revenue, the right to collect tolls, to operate a mill, etc., to some of his subjects, in return for which the subject became a vassal of the lord. He swore an oath of fealty binding him to the obligations of service and allegiance he had assumed. With such a contract he received ceremonial investiture from his lord.

These ceremonies establishing the relations between vassal and lord were almost identical with the process of naturalization in modern nation-states.

During the centuries of political feudalism, the actual government of the kings, the central power, was most rudimentary and primitive. Little, if any, direct relation existed between individual subjects and the central government of the king. Real power was vested in the feudal baron who was the actual ruler. He alone had control and power over the individuals.

The system, however, soon began to show its inadequacies. Within one large estate the lord of the land could provide his subjects with protection. But identical social units were developing in the same way on all sides, with corresponding power and rights vested in the neighboring barons. Hundreds, thousands of feudal lords obtained sovereign rights over their lands and over their subjects.

The relations between the lords and their subjects were established by custom and regulated by law, but the relationships between the neighboring lords of the land were unregulated except by family ties, friendships, pledges and agreements between them. Naturally, jealousies and rivalries soon flared up among the individual lords, who more and more frequently called upon their subjects to take up arms and fight the subjects of a neighboring lord to protect their own sovereignty, their lands, their influence.

As intercommunications developed and increased, as populations grew and interchange between feudal units was intensified, the conflicts between these units increased in frequency and violence. Each feudal knight looked upon the power and influence of his neighbors with fear, distrust and suspicion. There was no way to obtain security against attack other than to defeat one's neighbor in battle, conquer his lands, incorporate his subjects, thereby raising one's own power and widening one's own sphere of influence.

This evolution culminated in complete chaos with almost permanent fights between the various sovereign feudal units.

It took a long time for the subjects to realize that the contracts they had entered into with the feudal barons to obtain security and protection had brought them instead permanent wars, insecurity, misery and death. Finally, however, they found that their salvation could be achieved only by destroying the power of the feudal landlords and establishing and supporting a government to stand above the quarreling and warring barons, a government that would possess enough strength to create and enforce laws standing above feudal interests, and that would establish direct relations between the subjects and the central government, eliminating the intermediary feudal sovereignties. So they rallied around the kings, who became strong enough to impose a superior legal order.

Feudalism, a political system which dominated the world for five long centuries, finally began to disintegrate at the end of the thirteenth century, the moment better means of intercommunication and the growth of common ideas made wider centralization possible. Under the impact of these new conditions, the subjects turned against the sovereign feudal governments and established central governments under the sovereignty of the king, ending once and for all the interminable quarrels and fights between the intermediary social units which enslaved the population in the interest and for the maintenance of the sovereign power of the lords of the land.

What does this long and painful history of medieval society have to do with our problem in the twentieth century?

Man in society is constantly seeking security and freedom. This is a fundamental instinct. Both security and freedom are the products of law. Since history began to be written, the human race has struggled for the best forms and methods to achieve a social order within which man can have both freedom and security.

The historical evolution of human society proves that these human ideals are best achieved if the individual is in direct relationship with a supreme, central, universal source of law. Twice in the history of Western civilization this truth, which seems axiomatic, has found institutional expression: in the monotheistic religions and in democracy.

The fundamental doctrine of the Jewish, Christian and Mohammedan religions is monotheism, the oneness of God—the Supreme Lawgiver—the basic belief that before God, every man is equal. This doctrine, the rock upon which modern Western civilization is built, destroyed the polytheism of primitive human society. It destroyed the many different, selfish and inimical gods who, in the early stages of history, incited mankind to war and to destroy each other for the simple reason that every minor group of men had a different god whom they worshiped and who gave them law. The establishment of a single universal God as the Supreme Being and unique source of authority over mankind, and the attribution of His direct relationship to every man on earth, revealed for the first time the only lawmaking system upon which peaceful human society can be built.

At the time this elementary thesis of society was revealed and proclaimed, technical and material conditions were far too primitive to permit its application and effective realization in the known world. In religion, the doctrine slowly conquered the faith of man and became the dominating creed of the modern world. However, it could not assert itself as a political doctrine of a society that continued to develop along pre-Christian lines.

In the eighteenth century, political conditions at last induced the fathers of modern democracy to open a crusade to destroy the sovereignty of the many kings and rulers who oppressed and enslaved the people. This crusade led to the formulation and proclamation of the basic principle that sovereignty in human society resides in the community.

This principle, the very foundation of democracy, represents the political corollary of monotheism. Its triumph meant the acceptance by society of the thesis that there can be only one supreme sovereign source of law—the will of the community—and that, under this sovereign law guaranteeing security and freedom to man in society, every man is to be regarded as equal.

It is one of the great tragedies of history that the recognition and proclamation of this principle came a century too early.

When it became the dominating doctrine, the universality of sovereignty, the universality of law, the indivisibility of the sovereignty of the community as the supreme source of democratic law, was not yet feasible or technically possible. The world was still too big, it could not yet be centrally controlled, it was still an exclusively agricultural planet with economic conditions scarcely different from those of antiquity. So a substitute presented itself which permitted the new doctrine of democratic sovereignty to find immediate practical expression.

This substitute was the nation.

An intermediary between the individual and the universal conception of democratic society, the sovereignty of the community, had to be established in order to make the organization of society on a democratic basis immediately realizable. In the eighteenth century, society could not possibly be organized universally. Consequently, democracy could not be organized according to its fundamentally universal principles. It had to be organized nationally.

For a long time the problem seemed to have been satisfactorily solved and citizens and subjects of the modern democratic nation-states enjoyed a hitherto unknown degree of freedom, security and welfare. Relations between the nation-state and its citizens were stabilized, according to which the state guaranteed protection, security, law and order, in exchange for which the citizens pledged exclusive allegiance to their national state and agreed to accept its laws, to pay taxes and to go to battle when national interests required the supreme sacrifice.

The national organization of democracy worked perfectly well—for a while. But soon, under the impetus of technical, scientific and economic developments, and the tremendous increase of intercommunication, interchange of ideas, populations and production, the various sovereign national units were brought into close contact with each other. Just as in the medieval age, these contacts between the sovereign national units—the relationships of which were unregulated—created frictions and conflicts.

Today we find ourselves in the same social convulsion and political chaos that human society was passing through at the end of the thirteenth century. Far from enjoying freedom, far from obtaining the expected security and protection from their nation-states, the citizens are constantly exposed to oppression, violence and destruction. The multiplicity of the conflicting sovereign units in our society destroys every vestige of the freedom, protection and security originally promised and granted to the individual by the nation-states at their inception in the eighteenth century.

In the middle of the twentieth century, we are living in an era of absolute political feudalism in which the nation-states have assumed exactly the same roles as were assumed by the feudal barons a thousand years ago.

Feudalism created serfdom, not because the supreme source of law was an individual or a family, but because in a given territory there were *many* individuals and families exercising sovereign power and because these various sovereign units were not brought under a higher, all-embracing law. The fact that men were living in a society composed of a multiplicity of scattered and disintegrated sovereignties, led feudalism into a series of conflagrations which caused the utter misery and starvation of the peoples and the ultimate self-destruction of the system.

The fact that today we are not ruled by barons and counts but by institutions created by national constitutions, loses its significance when the multiplicity of such scattered sovereign institutions divides mankind into separate sovereign units. This arbitrary and artificial segregation of human society compels nation-states to act in exactly the same way toward their subjects and toward their neighbors that feudal lords of the land acted under similar conditions to uphold their symbols and institutions, their power and influence, which were for them absolute, ultimate ends.

There is nothing kings, emperors or tyrants ever did to their subjects that nation-states are not doing today. Tyranny does not mean the rule of a king, emperor, dictator or despot. It is to live under a system of law in the creation of which the individual does not participate.

In the nation-state system, we are unable to participate in the creation of law in any part of human society beyond our own country. It is, therefore, a self-delusion to say that Americans, Englishmen or Frenchmen are "free people." They can be attacked by other nations and forced into war at any time. They are living in a state of fear and insecurity just as great as under tyrants who interfered with their liberties at will.

Absolute monarchy was anti-democratic and tyrannical, not because it was wicked or malevolent, but because it identified the interests of the king with the interests of the people over whom he ruled and because it acted solely to safeguard its particular interests.

This is exactly the position of the present-day nation-states. Guided exclusively by their own national interests, disregarding completely the interests of their fellow states and having sovereign power in their respective countries, the nation-states have become anti-democratic and have re-established the absolutism our forefathers destroyed when it was personified by kings.

If we take human society as a whole—which in relation to technological reality is smaller today than the society over which the Carlovingian kings ruled—we have to admit that we are living in a society without public law. The legislation of the various nation-states dividing humanity into a number of closed and separated units has all the characteristics of the private law of the medieval dukes, counts and barons, which usurped public law for so many centuries, creating immeasurable bloodshed and misery for all who lived under this multiplicity of distinct systems of law.

This system of nation-feudalism has plunged the world into unprecedented barbarism, and destroyed almost all individual rights and human liberties

secured with so much toil and blood by our forefathers. Modern nation-feudalism has erased,
except in name, every moral doctrine of Christianity.

There is not the slightest hope that we can
change the course into which we are rapidly being
driven by the conflicting nation-states so long as
we recognize them as the supreme and final expression of the sovereignty of the people. At ever-
increasing speed we shall be hurled toward
greater insecurity, greater destruction, greater hatred, greater barbarism, greater misery, until we
resolve to destroy the political system of nation-
feudalism and establish a social order based on the
sovereignty of the community, as conceived by the
founders of democracy and as it applies to the
realities of today.

This necessitates the realization and acceptance
of the following axioms:

1. Individual freedom and individual security in
   modern society are the product of democratically created and democratically executed
   law.
2. All individuals must be directly related to the
   institutions expressing the sovereignty of the
   community.
3. Any intermediary organizations with attributes of sovereignty standing between individuals and the institutions of the sovereignty of the community (cities, provinces,
   churches, nations or any other units) destroy
   the rights of the individual, the sovereignty of

the community and, consequently, destroy democracy itself.

CHAPTER VII

WHAT IS WAR?

I T IS commonly taken for granted that we can never abolish war between nations, because war is in the nature of man. It is even more widely accepted that war has innumerable causes and that to try to abolish all of them would be a hopeless task.

We must refuse to accept such apparently true but basically deceptive statements, if we would avoid becoming the helpless victims of superstition. No one knows just what "human nature" is. Nor is this a relevant question. Assuming or even admitting that certain evils *are* part of "human nature," this does not mean that we should sit passively and refuse to investigate the conditions which cause the evils to become deadly and the possibility of avoiding their devastating effects.

Since man began to think about life and himself, it has been generally accepted that appendicitis and gallstones were in the nature of man. Indeed, they are. But after thousands of years, during which men died for these fatal evils of "human nature," some people had the courage to take a knife and cut open the diseased part to see what was happening. Appendicitis and gallstones continue to be "in the nature of man." But now man does not necessarily die from them.

Superficially, it looks as though wars have been waged for a great variety of reasons. The struggle for food and mere survival among primitive tribes, feuds between families and dynasties, quarrels between cities and provinces, religious fanaticism, rival commercial interests, antagonistic social ideals, the race for colonies, economic competition and many other forces have exploded in fatal and devastating wars.

Since time immemorial, among primitive people, families, clans and tribes have fought, enslaved and exterminated each other for food, shelter, women, pastures, hunting grounds. Each group had a "religion," a demon, a totem, a god, or several of each, whose divine and supreme will was interpreted by priests, medicine men and magicians, and who protected them from the dangers and depredations of other clans; inspired and incited them to war upon and to annihilate their neighbors. Life at that stage of society was no different from the life of fish in the deep and beasts in the jungle.

Later, at a higher level of civilization, we see larger settlements and city communities fighting and warring with each other. Nineveh, Babylon, Troy, Cnossos, Athens, Sparta, Rome, Carthage and many other similar rival settlements continuously battled, until all of them were finally destroyed.

Under the inspiration and leadership of dynamic personalities, powerful clans and races set out upon wars of conquest so that they might rule over new lands and subjects in safety and wealth. Tiglath Pileser, Nebuchadnezzar, Darius, Alexander, Attila, Genghis Khan and other conquerors in history waged large-scale wars to subdue the world as it was known to them.

For centuries after the fall of Rome, European society was rocked by endless clashes and battles among thousands of feudal barons.

After the consolidation of the three world religions originating in Judaism—Catholicism, Islamism and Protestantism—a long series of wars were fought by the followers of these expanding and conflicting faiths. Kings, princes and knights took part in crusades to defend and spread their own creeds, to destroy and exterminate the believers in the other creeds. The great wars fought by Constantine, Charles V, Suleiman, Phillip II, Gustavus Adolphus and other mighty rulers of the Middle Ages were mostly attempts to unify the Western world under one religion.

Following the collapse of the feudal system, with the development of craftsmanship, trade and shipping, a middle class of modern bourgeois citizenry emerged and began to crystallize. The field of conflict again shifted, and wars were fought by great commercial centers, Venice, Florence, Augsburg, Hamburg, Amsterdam, Ghent, Danzig and other city units, which impressed their own citizens and hired mercenaries.

Then another series of wars were waged by absolute monarchs in the interest of their dynasties, to widen the domains of the great royal houses. The Hapsburg, Bourbon, Wittelsbach, Romanoff and Stuart monarchies and dozens of minor dynasties led their subjects into battle to defend and extend their power and rule.

A different type of war was waged between smaller kingdoms and principalities to obtain supremacy within a particular system of monarchy, such as the wars between England and Scotland; Saxony, Bavaria and Prussia; Tuscany, Piedmont and Parma; Burgundy, Touraine and Normandy.

And finally, the creation of modern nation-states at the end of the eighteenth century has brought about a series of gigantic conflicts between whole conscripted nations, culminating in the first and second world wars.

Looking back over history, war appears a hundred-headed hydra. As soon as the peacemakers chop off one head, new ones immediately appear on the monster. Yet, if we analyze what seem to be the manifold causes of past wars, it is not difficult to observe a thread of continuity running through these strange historical phenomena.

Why did cities once wage wars against each other and why do municipalities no longer fight each other with weapons today? Why, at certain times, have great landowner barons warred with each other and why have they now ceased that practice? Why did the various churches plunge their adherents into armed warfare and why today are they able to worship side by side without shooting each other? Why did Scotland and England, Saxony and Prussia, Parma and Tuscany, at a certain period in their history, go to battle against each other and why have they ceased fighting today?

A careful study of human history reveals that the assumption that war is inherent in human nature—and therefore eternal—is shallow and faulty, that it is only a superficial impression. Far from being inexplicable or inevitable, we can invariably determine the situations that predispose to war, and the conditions which lead to war.

The real cause of all wars has always been the same. They have occurred with the mathematical regularity of a natural law at clearly determined moments as the result of clearly definable conditions.

If we try to detect the mechanism visibly in operation, the single cause ever-present at the outbreak of each and every conflict known to human history, if we attempt to reduce the seemingly innumerable causes of war to a common denominator, two clear and unmistakable observations emerge.

1. Wars between groups of men forming social units always take place when these units— tribes, dynasties, churches, cities, nations—

exercise unrestricted sovereign power.
2. Wars between these social units cease the moment sovereign power is transferred from them to a larger or higher unit.

From these observations we can deduce a social law with the characteristics of an axiom that applies to and explains each and every war in the history of all time.

War takes place whenever and wherever non-integrated social units of equal sovereignty come into contact.

War between given social units of equal sovereignty is the permanent symptom of each successive phase of civilization. Wars always ceased when a higher unit established its own sovereignty, absorbing the sovereignties of the conflicting smaller social groups. After such transfers of sovereignty, a period of peace followed, which lasted only until the new social units came into contact. Then a new series of wars began.

The causes and reasons alleged by history to have brought about these conflicts are irrelevant, as they continued to exist long after the wars had ceased. Cities and provinces continue to compete with each other. Religious convictions are just as different today as they were during the religious wars.

The only thing that did change was the institutionalization of sovereignty, the transfer of sovereignty from one type of social unit to another and a higher one.

Just as there is one and only one cause for wars

between men on this earth, so history shows that peace—not peace in an absolute and utopian sense, but concrete peace between given social groups warring with each other at given times—has always been established in one way and only in one way.

Peace between fighting groups of men was never possible and wars succeeded one another until some sovereignty, some sovereign source of law, some sovereign power was set up *over* and *above* the clashing social units, integrating the warring units into a higher sovereignty.

Once the mechanics and the fundamental causes of wars—of all wars—are realized, the futility and childishness of the passionate debates about armament and disarmament must be apparent to all.

If human society were organized so that relations between groups and units in contact were regulated by democratically controlled law and legal institutions, then modern science could go ahead, devise and produce the most devastating weapons, and there would be no war. But if we allow sovereign rights to reside in the separate units and groups without regulating their relations by law, then we can prohibit every weapon, even a penknife, and people will beat out each other's brains with clubs.

It is tragic to witness the utter blindness and ignorance of our governments and political leaders in regard to this all-important and vital problem of the world.

Voices are now being raised in the United States

and in Great Britain demanding compulsory military service and the maintenance of extensive armaments in peacetime. The argument is that if in 1939 the United States and Great Britain had been armed, Germany and Japan would never have dared to start a war. The Western democracies must not be caught unprepared again. If conscription is introduced and America and England have large armed forces ready to fight at a moment's notice, no other power will dare attack them, and they will not be forced into war. That sounds logical. But what about France, the Soviet Union, Belgium, Czechoslovakia, Yugoslavia and the other countries which always had conscription and large standing armies? Did this save them from war?

After 1919, the peacemakers were obsessed by the idea that armaments lead to wars, that a *sine qua non* for world peace is the general limitation and reduction of armaments on sea, land and in the air. Disarmament completely dominated international thought for fifteen years after the signature of the Covenant. Tremendous amounts of propaganda were poured into the public ear by printed and spoken word, to the effect that "armament manufacturers" were the real culprits responsible for wars, that no nation should build battleships bigger than thirty-five thousand tons, that the caliber of guns should be reduced, submarine and gas warfare prohibited, military service shortened, and so forth.

These views found the democratic victors

receptive and persuaded them to disarm to a large extent. But naturally they were without effect on the vanquished who sought revenge and a revision of the *status quo* by force. The outbreak of the second World War proved conclusively the complete fallacy and uselessness of seeking peace between nations through disarmament.

Now our leaders are preaching the exact opposite. We are told today that only powerful armaments can maintain peace, that the democratic and so-called peace-loving nations must maintain omnipotent national navies, air forces and mechanized armies, that we must control strategic military bases spread around the globe, if we would prevent aggression and maintain peace.

This idea, the idea of maintaining peace by armaments, is just as complete a fallacy as the idea of maintaining peace through disarmament. Technical equipment, arms, have as much to do with peace as frogs with the weather. Conscription and large armies are just as incapable of maintaining peace as no conscription and disarmament.

The problem of peace is a social and political problem, not a technical one.

War is never the disease itself. War is a reaction to a disease of society, the symptom of disease. It is just like fever in the human body. We shall never be able to prevent all wars in advance, because it is impossible to foresee future differentiations of human society, exactly where divisions and splits of society will take place. In the twenty-fifth century perhaps the great conflict will be between the orange growers and the believers in Taoism. We do not know.

What we do know is that war is the result of contact between nonintegrated sovereign units, whether such units be families, tribes, villages, estates, cities, provinces, dynasties, religions, classes, nations, regions or continents.

We also know that today, the conflict is between the scattered units of nation-states. During the past hundred years, all major wars have been waged between nations. This division among men is the only condition which, in our age, can create—and undoubtedly will create—other wars.

The task therefore is to prevent wars between the nations—international wars.

Logical thinking and historical empiricism agree that there *is* a way to solve this problem and prevent wars between the nations once and for all. But with equal clarity they also reveal that there is *one* way and one way alone to achieve this end: The integration of the scattered conflicting national sovereignties into one unified, higher sovereignty, capable of creating a legal order within which all peoples may enjoy equal security, equal obligations and equal rights under law.

CHAPTER VIII

THE HISTORICAL MEANING OF SOVEREIGNTY

THE fundamental problem of peace is the problem of sovereignty. The welfare, the happiness, the very existence of a miner in Pennsylvania, Wales, Lorraine or the Don Basin, a farmer in the Ukraine, the Argentine, the American Middle West or the Chinese rice fields—the very existence of every individual or family in every country of the five continents depends upon the correct interpretation and application of sovereignty. This is not a theoretical debate but a question more vital than wages, prices, taxes, food or any other major issue of immediate interest to the common man everywhere, because in the final analysis, the solution of all the everyday problems of two thousand million human beings depends upon the solution of the central problem of war. And whether we are to have war or peace and progress depends upon whether we can create proper institutions to insure the security of the peoples.

Schopenhauer pointed out that health is a negative feeling of which we are never aware, while pain produces a positive sensation. If we cut our little finger, we concentrate on that completely dominating pain, excluding from our consciousness the many other parts of our body which remain uninjured and healthy.

This observation has also been proved true in other fields of human activity—certainly in the field of social science. Great social and political structures and revolutionary ideas are usually born in times of crisis.

The very fact that today there is so much talk of sovereignty—a word that was hardly mentioned in political discussions a decade or two ago—proves the existence of a sore spot in the body politic. It leaves no doubt that something is wrong with sovereignty, that the present interpretation of this notion is passing through a crisis and that clarification, restatement and reinterpretation are necessary.

In discussing this most intricate problem, it is essential to make a clear distinction between its two entirely different aspects.

The first is scientific: a realization of exactly what sovereignty is, what it meant historically during the various phases of human development, and what it means in a democracy in the middle of the twentieth century.

The second—which we must *eliminate* from consideration while searching for definitions and principles is: What would the people be capable of understanding, and what would they accept politically right now?

In our endeavor to arrive at a clear definition and correct interpretation of democratic sovereignty, we must not be deterred by the argument that the quest is futile because the people are nationalist and would resist any changes in the present political construction of the world. Such an outlook—a sort of government by polls of public opinion—is not democracy, but its caricature.

New ideas always take shape within a small group of men whose task it is to spread them and get them accepted by the people.

When Pasteur discovered that contagious diseases were caused by living organisms and explained how such diseases could be cured, almost everybody, including the overwhelming majority of doctors, laughed at him. At the time Hertz and Marconi declared that sound and signals could be transmitted around the world by radio waves, a public opinion poll would certainly have shown that ninety-nine per cent of the people believed such a thing impossible and for all purposes, impractical. Those who, at the time of the Thirty Years' War, declared that it was possible for Catholics and Protestants to worship in freedom according to their beliefs and to live together peacefully under law, were regarded as dreamers and most impractical men.

Democracy does not mean that governments have to ask the people their opinions on complicated issues and then carry them out. It is essentially a form of society within which the conception of new ideas, their diffusion in view of their acceptance by the majority, the fight for leadership, is open to everybody.

The first problem, therefore, is that those who,

for one reason or another, are in a position to influence public opinion and events should know the exact meaning of the words they are using and clearly define the ideas they are advocating.

The first step toward realism is the clarification of principles.

It seems one of the absurdities of our unhappy generation that hopeless utopians who live entirely in the past and are incapable of visualizing the future otherwise than as a projection of the past, call themselves realists and practical men and deride any attempt at rational thinking as "idealism."

What does this word "sovereignty" mean?

By now most people must realize that human beings are exceptionally perverted and ferocious creatures, capable of murdering, torturing, persecuting and exploiting each other more ruthlessly than any other species in this world.

At a very early stage of human society, it was discovered that before we could live together, in a family, in a tribe, it was necessary to impose certain restraints upon our natural impulses, to forbid certain things we like to do, and to compel us to do certain things we do not like to do.

The day the first legal imposition of a compulsion was forced upon a community was the greatest day in history.

That day, freedom was born.

How did this happen?

Human nature is such that man does not accept rules unless they are imposed upon him by constituted authority. The first absolute authority was

God.

So it was necessary to make people believe that the required rules and regulations were the express commands of God. They were proclaimed with all the magic at their command by priests, who had direct access to God and who knew how to proclaim His will, amid so much thunder and lightning that the people were frightened into accepting them.

Here we have the first sovereign authority—the first source of law—a supernatural symbol.

Later on as human society developed and law and order grew, it was necessary to separate that which was Caesar's from that which was God's. During that long period of history when peoples were ruled by the divine right of absolute monarchs, chiefs, emperors and kings, to maintain their authority and lawmaking power, to make people recognize them as the supreme source of law, the rulers linked themselves as closely as possible with religion and proclaimed that they derived their power from God.

The monarchs ruling by divine right were called sovereigns and their lawgiving capacity was designated as "sovereign."

Between the Renaissance and the eighteenth century, as a result of the revival of learning and new methods of rational and scientific thinking, a revolutionary social ideal took shape and found fertile soil among the masses suffering under absolutism. This revolutionary ideal was the principle that no individual, no family, no dynasty, could any longer be regarded as sovereign, that the sovereign lawgiving authority was the people and that "sovereignty resides in the community."

This revolutionary principle led to the great popular uprisings of the eighteenth century, to the establishment of the American and French republics, and to the "king reigns but does not rule" parliamentary system in England and many other countries.

The ideal of national sovereignty and national independence springs from long eras of monarchy and colonization. At its inception, it was a great forward step and an incentive to human progress. The American Declaration of Independence, the French Revolution, following on the development of representative institutions in England, were an enormous incentive to other peoples to fight for their own sovereignty and independence. The climax of this evolution was reached in the peace treaties of 1919, when more nations than ever before became completely sovereign and independent. Twenty years late all those proud national sovereignties lay trampled in the dust and today more people than ever before in modern history are enslaved and plunged into misery.

Why did this happen?

It happened because the political system established in 1919, an apotheosis of eighteenth century ideals, was an anachronism, and in total contradiction to things as they are in the twentieth century. The great ideals of national sovereignty, independence, nationality as the basis of states, were wonderful achievements in the eighteenth century, in a world which was so vast before the industrial revolution had begun.

The democratic form of government adopted by the great Western powers brought about a century of wealth, a spiritual, scientific and material progress unique in history. But nothing is eternal in this world, and we are again in the throes of a crisis which demands reinterpretation of the foundations of our social life.

Our present conception of national sovereignty shows how an ideal once realized, can be distorted in the span of a single century.

According to the eighteenth century French philosophers, the most articulate among the founders of modern democracy, the democratic conception of sovereignty meant the transfer of sovereign rights from one man, the king; to all men, the people. In the democratic sense, sovereignty resided in the community.

By "community" they meant the totality of people. It was quite clear that no individual or groups of individuals could exercise sovereign rights unless *derived* from the sovereignty of the community.

We must try to visualize the world as it was in the eighteenth century. The industrial revolution had not even begun. The stagecoach was the fastest means of transportation. Everybody lived a rural life and any territory of one hundred thousand or even ten thousand square miles was an entirely self-sufficient and self-supporting unit.

Under such conditions, the widest horizon of the forebears of democracy was—the Nation. When they proclaimed the sovereignty of the nation, they meant the sovereignty of the community; they meant sovereignty to have the broadest possible basis.

Today, a hundred and fifty years later, when we can fly around the globe in less time than it took to go from Boston to New York, from London to Glasgow or from Paris to Marseille, the situation is completely different.

As the world is organized today, sovereignty does *not* reside in the community, but is exercised in an absolute form by groups of individuals we call nations. This is in total contradiction to the original democratic conception of sovereignty. To-day, sovereignty has far too narrow a basis; it no longer has the power it should and was meant to have. The word is the same. The conception it expresses is the same. But the surroundings have changed. The conditions of the world have changed. And this changed situation calls for corresponding changes in the interpretation of this basic principle, if we desire to preserve this, the only foundation of democratic society yet discovered.

The great change brought about by the technical and industrial achievements of the nineteenth century is that the nation, which in the eighteenth century was the *broadest* imaginable basis of sovereignty, today is far too *narrow* a basis.

The seeds of the twentieth century crisis began to germinate almost immediately after the establishment of the modern democratic nation-states. Quite independently of the organization of the nation-states and the political conceptions of eighteenth century democracy, almost at the same time something happened which was destined to become an equally strong movement and an equally powerful factor of human progress. That something was: Industrialism.

These two dominating currents of our age, nationalism and industrialism, are in constant and inevitable conflict with each other.

Industrialism tends to embrace the whole globe within its sphere of activity. Modern industrial mass production needs raw materials from all over the earth, and seeks markets in every corner of the world. It strives to achieve its purposes irrespective of any political, geographic, racial, religious, linguistic or national barriers.

Nationalism, on the other hand, tends to divide this world into smaller and smaller compartments and to segregate the human race into smaller and smaller independent groups.

For about a century it was possible for these conflicting currents to flow side by side. The political constitution of the eighteenth century nation-state structure of the world had some compartments large enough for industrialism to develop.

But since the beginning of this century these two forces have clashed with titanic violence. It is this collision between our political life and our economic and technological life that is the cause of the twentieth century crisis with which we have been struggling since 1914, as helpless as guinea pigs.

The meaning of this convulsion is clear. The political framework of our world with its seventy or eighty sovereign nation-states is an insurmountable obstacle to free industrial progress, to individual liberty and to social security.

Either we understand this problem and create a political framework in this world within which industrialism, individual liberties and peaceful human relationship are possible or we dogmatically refuse to change the foundation of our obsolete political structure.

We *can* remain as we are. It is perfectly possible. But if this is our choice, then democracy is finished and we are bound to march with increasing speed toward totalitarianism.

The first step toward ending the present chaos is to overcome the tremendous emotional obstacle which prevents us from realizing and admitting that the ideal of sovereign nation-states, with all its great record of success during the nineteenth century, is today the cause of all the immeasurable suffering and misery of this world. We are living in complete anarchy, because in a small world, interrelated in every other respect, there are seventy or eighty separate sources of law—seventy or eighty sovereignties.

The situation is identical with that period of history when feudal lords of the land had absolute sovereign power over their fiefs and spent their lives fighting and killing each other, until the over-all rulers, the kings, imposed a higher sovereignty upon them, based on a broader framework. Within such a broader framework, the knights continued to envy and to dislike each other. But they were obliged to envy and dislike each other—peacefully.

Our present system of national sovereignty is in absolute contradiction to the original democratic conception of sovereignty, which meant—and still means—sovereignty of the community.

Why is it so urgently necessary to revive this notion and to re-establish the democratic conception of sovereignty of the community, which means authority of the people, standing *above* any individual or any group of individuals?

We all reject the monstrous totalitarian conception that the state is the absolute ultimate goal, with supreme power over its citizens, that the individual is merely the abject slave of the Moloch—state.

We accept the democratic conception that the state, created by the people, exists only to protect them and maintain law and order, safeguarding their lives and liberty.

The significant thing about the present crisis is that the nation-states, even the most powerful, even the United States of America, Great Britain and the Soviet Union, are no longer strong enough, no longer powerful enough to fulfill the purpose for which they were created.

They cannot prevent disasters like the first and second world wars. They cannot protect their peoples against the devastation of international war.

However sincerely the American, British and Russian governments sought to keep out of this war, they were forced into it in spite of themselves. Millions of their citizens have died, hundreds of billions of dollars of their national wealth have been wasted, for sheer survival. They had to fight for their lives.

If the sovereignty of the United States of America, the sovereignty of Great Britain and the sovereignty of the Soviet Union do not suffice to protect their citizens, then we need not even talk about the fiction of sovereignty in Latvia, Luxembourg or Rumania.

To put it plainly, the ideal of the nation-state is bankrupt. The nation-state is impotent to prevent foreign aggression, it no longer serves as the supreme institution capable of protecting its people against war and all the miseries and misfortunes that war brings.

The second World War has finally demonstrated that not a single one of the existing nations, even the most powerful, is economically self-sufficient.

These indisputable facts prove that our present conception of national sovereignty is obsolete and pregnant with deadly danger to us all.

The inescapable economic and technical realities of our age make it imperative to re-examine and reinterpret the notion of sovereignty and to create sovereign institutions based on the community, according to the original democratic conception. Sovereignty of the people must stand *above* the nations so that under it each nation may be equal, just as each individual is equal under the law in a civilized state.

The question is not one of "surrendering" national sovereignty. The problem is not negative and does not involve giving up something we already have. The problem is positive—creating something we lack, something we have never had, but that we imperatively need.

The creation of institutions with universal sovereign power is merely another phase of the same process in the development of human history—the extension of law and order into another field of human association which heretofore has remained unregulated and in anarchy.

A few centuries ago, many cities held full sovereign rights. Later some portion of municipal sovereignty was transferred to provinces. Then to larger units and finally, at the end of the eighteenth century, to the nation-states.

In the United States of America today, the problems of fire prevention, water supply, street cleaning and other similar matters are under municipal authority.

The construction of roads, marital legislation, education, legislation regarding industrial and commercial enterprises, and endless other issues are under state sovereignty.

And finally, problems affecting the United States

Army, Navy, foreign policy, currency and other matters, are under Federal sovereignty.

The development is crystal clear. As human progress continues, conditions require an ever-broader basis for sovereignty, for absolute power, to fulfill its purpose: the protection of the people.

New Yorkers are citizens of the city of New York, of the state of New York and of the United States of America. But they are also citizens of the world. Their lives, their security, their liberties are protected in a very wide field by the sovereign authority which resides in the people, who have delegated its exercise partly to the city of New York, partly to the state of New York and partly to the Federal government of the United States of America.

The situation as to the delegation of sovereign power by the people to authorities on different levels is the same in all democratic countries. Just as in the United States, so in Great Britain, France, Switzerland and in the other countries, the sovereign peoples have delegated parts of their sovereignties to municipalities, boroughs, counties, departments, cantons and national state institutions.

But during the past three decades, we have learned that these highest sovereign units created by the people—the nation-states—are not strong enough, are not sovereign enough, to protect them against international war, against attack by a foreign power over which existing sovereignties have no control whatever.

If the state of New York enacted economic or social legislation that reacted harmfully on economic and labor conditions in Connecticut, and no higher sovereignty existed, such an act on the part of the sovereign state of New York could not be prevented by the sovereign state of Connecticut, except by war.

But a higher sovereignty—the Federal sovereignty—exists, and under it the state of New York and the state of Connecticut are equal. This higher sovereignty alone protects the people against such danger.

The same dangers would exist in the relations of counties in England, departments in France and cantons in Switzerland, without higher sovereign national authority.

Democratic sovereignty of the people can be correctly expressed and effectively instituted only if local affairs are handled by local government, national affairs by national government, and international, world affairs, by international, world government.

Only if the people, in whom rests all sovereign power, delegate parts of their sovereignty to institutions created for and capable of dealing with specific problems, can we say that we have a democratic form of government. Only through such separation of sovereignties, through the organization of independent institutions, deriving their authority from the sovereignty of the community, can we have a social order in which men may live in peace with each other, endowed with equal rights and equal obligations before law. Only in a world order based on such separation of sovereignties can individual freedom be real.

Such separation of sovereignties, such gradation of governmental functions, has proved to be the only real, enduring instrument of democracy in any country.

It is irrelevant whether the delegation of sovereignty proceeds from local government to national government, as in the United States, or from national government to local government, as in Great Britain. Whether the delegation of sovereignty develops historically one way or the other, does not modify the fact that democracy needs separation of sovereignties and separate institutions to deal with affairs on different levels, adequately to express the sovereignty of the community.

Existing anarchy in international relations, due to absolute national sovereignty, must be superseded by universal statutory law, enacted by a duly elected legislative body. Such universal law must take the place of the utterly fallacious, ineffectual and precarious rule of unenforceable treaty obligations entered into by sovereign nation-states and disregarded by them whenever it suits their purpose.

The conception of sovereignty is not an end but a means to an end.

It is an instrument necessary to create law and order in the relations of men. Sovereignty finds expression in institutions, but in itself, is not and never can be identical with any institution.

Institutions derive their sovereignty from where sovereignty resides. In ancient times, in religion, in absolute monarchies—from God. In democracies—from the people.

If our inherited institutions, established in the past, are no longer capable of maintaining law and order and protecting us, then their claims to sovereignty, their insistence upon sovereign power jeopardizes our very lives and liberty, the well-being of society to which we belong, and the sovereignty of... "we, the people."

Institutions—churches, dynasties, municipalities, kingdoms, nation-states—can be recognized to exercise sovereign power and to incarnate sovereign rights only so long as they are able to solve concrete and tangible problems, to fulfill the purposes for which they were created. To identify sovereign institutions with sovereignty itself, to assume that sovereign rights must eternally reside in any specific institution—today the nation-state—to believe that the nation-state is *the* expression of sovereignty, is pure totalitarianism, the greatest foe of democracy, the greatest political and social heresy imaginable, ranking with the making of graven images of God and their identification with God Himself in the Christian religion.

The nation-states were originally instituted and received their power from their peoples to carry out clearly defined tasks, i.e., to protect their citizens, to guarantee security to their peoples, to maintain law and order. The moment established institutions fail to keep abreast of conditions in society and are unable to maintain peace, they become a source of great danger and must be reformed if violent social convulsions and wars are to be averted.

Through such reform and transformation of obsolete and ineffective human institutions into more adequate and more powerful institutions adapted to realities, nothing whatsoever is "sacrificed" or "surrendered." Quite certainly not sovereignty.

Such a reform does not require the abolition of nations and national boundaries. Within each nation-state, we still have state lines, county demarcations, city limits, boundaries of our home lots or of houses and apartments. Families have names of their own different from those of other families. We like, protect and defend our own families more than other families. We love our homes, pay allegiance to our own communities, our countrysides, our provinces.

But sovereign power is not vested in these units which divide us.

Sovereign power is vested in the state, which unites us.

Those who talk of "surrendering" the sovereignty of the United States, of Great Britain, France or of any other democratic country, simply do not understand the meaning of "sovereignty."

A democratic state cannot "surrender" sovereignty, for the simple reason that it is not sovereign. Only a totalitarian or Fascist state is sovereign. A democratic state is sovereign only to the extent to which sovereignty is delegated to it by those in whom, under the democratic concept, sovereignty is vested—the people.

The real source of sovereign power cannot be emphasized too strongly and must never be lost sight of if we would understand the political problem we face. It is the people who create governments and not—as the Fascists say—governments that make nations.

The nation-states as they were set up in the eighteenth century, and as they are organized in the democracies today, are nothing but the instruments of the sovereign people, created for the specific purpose of achieving certain objectives. Should the people realize and come to the conclusion that in certain fields they would be better protected by delegating part of their sovereignty to bodies other than the nation-states, then nothing would be "surrendered." Rather something would be created for the better protection of the lives and liberties of all peoples.

Sovereignty would continue to reside in the people in accordance with the original conception of democracy, but institutions would be created to give realistic and effective expression to the democratic sovereignty of the people in place of the inefficient and tyrannical institutions of the nation-states.

The people would "surrender" their sovereignty only if sovereign power to create law were abandoned to an arbitrary authority or a lawless power.

But to transfer certain aspects of our sovereign rights from national legislative, judiciary and executive bodies to equally democratically elected and democratically controlled universal legislative, judiciary and executive bodies in order to create, apply and execute law for the regulation of human relationships in the international field—in a field where such law has never existed—is not "surrender" but *acquisition*. It is an exchange of a phantom asset, the product of unfulfilled and unfulfillable promises, for a real and tangible asset.

CHAPTER IX

TREATY OR LAW

I F AT any time since the Tower of Babel utter confusion has reigned in this world, it is today—confusion created by discussion of the why and wherefore of the second World War and of the conditions and possibilities of peace. Thousands of books and articles have been published and speeches made about the all-important problem confronting us: how to establish a world order that will prevent another global war.

All the planners of lasting peace believe that theirs is the magic formula; that they can make something work which never has worked; that after the failure of thousands of peace treaties they can draft one that will prevent war.

What caused these world wars?

Again and again we must raise this question to see clearly the anatomy of peace, because only by accurate diagnosis can we find a cure and arrive at a healthier international life.

As an explanation of the second World War, no reasonable man can accept Hitler or Mussolini, or Fascism, totalitarianism, or Japanese militarism, or French corruption, or Bolshevism, or British appeasement, or American isolationism. These and many other explanations are easily accessible sand piles in which to bury our heads like ostriches; they are convenient self-justifications for our delusion that we are the innocent victims of circumstances and of the malice and mischief of others. They tell nothing at all of the why and wherefore of the second World War.

That war came because our social institutions and principles—as we inherited them and as we worship them today—are in total contradiction to economic, technical and scientific realities of the twentieth century in which we live.

Our democratic national constitutions, the result of slow ideological development, of a long and laborious upward struggle, with much shedding of blood, and revolutions not a few, were drawn up by our forebears who lived under primitive, rural conditions. The laws and institutions they created were determined by the conditions in which they lived.

The institutions established and the standards

set by our eighteenth century forebears opened up a century of unprecedented progress and prosperity. More can hardly be expected from human institutions. Conditions that have arisen since the birth of this century, however, have made it impossible for those institutions to control and channel the torrent of events, the force and scope of which could not be foreseen at the time national institutions were created.

Our leading statesmen and political thinkers, puzzled by the events of the first half of the twentieth century and unable to understand the essence of peace, seek to escape responsibility by taking refuge in such nebulous assertions as: "It is impossible to foresee what the situation will be in twenty years..." or "We cannot at this time prescribe rules of conduct for future behavior..." Consequently, they argue, let us seek a "temporary" solution, a "provisional" settlement for a "cooling-off period," for a "transitional" period, after which—"we shall see..."

Looking back five thousand years, it can be seen that every decade, every year, every day, has always been a "transitional period." Human history is nothing but an endless chain of "transitions." Transition is the only permanent thing on this earth. In human affairs the temporary is the perpetual.

The problem of peace is not to create a permanent *status quo*. It is to pass through these endless changes and transitions by methods other than violence.

We have always been able to solve the problem of peace *within* sovereign groups of men. We have never been able to solve this very same problem of peace *between* sovereign groups of men, today between nations. The reason is obvious.

Trying to solve international problems by diplomacy or foreign policy, through alliances or the balance of power, is like attempting to cure cancer with aspirin.

We could not have a peaceful society in any country if it were based on the idea that the Jones or the Smith family should enter into an agreement with the Al Capone family or Jack the Ripper family, pledging peaceful relationship among themselves.

Peace in a society means that relations among the members of the society are regulated by law, that there is a democratically controlled machinery of lawmaking, of jurisdiction, and that to carry out these laws the community has the right to use force, a right which is denied to the individual members of that community.

Peace is order based on law. There is no other imaginable definition.

Any other conception of peace is sheer utopia.

Each time a war is fought, it is followed by endless debate on the kind of peace treaty that will be made. Hundreds of suggestions are advanced, but no matter what kind of treaty is signed, the next war is inevitable.

Why?

Because the content of a treaty is irrelevant—

the treaty idea itself is at fault.

We have had thousands and thousands of peace treaties in the history of mankind. None of them has survived for more than a few years. None of them could prevent the next war, for the simple reason that human nature, which cannot be changed, is such that conflicts are inevitable as long as sovereign power resides in individual members or groups of members of society, and not in society itself.

Quite certainly peace is not a utopia.

The only question is, what kind of peace?

If we seek peace between x sovereign units, based on treaty agreements, then peace is an impossibility and it is childish even to think of it. But if we conceive peace correctly, as order based on law, then peace is a practical proposition that can be realized just as well between the nation-states as it has been realized so often in the past among states, provinces, cities, principalities and other units.

Whether we are to have peace or continually recurring war depends on a very simple proposition.

It depends upon whether we want to base international relations on treaties or on law.

If the second World War is again followed by another treaty or covenant, the next war may be taken for granted. If we have the foresight, and decide to make that fundamental and revolutionary change in human history, to try to introduce law into the regulation of international relations, then and not until then shall we approach an order which may be called "peace."

The reason for this is not difficult to understand.

The essence of life is constant change, perpetual development.

Up to now, peace between nations has always been a static conception. We have always tried to determine some sort of *status quo,* to seal it meticulously in a treaty, and to make any change in that *status quo* impossible except through war.

This is a grotesque misconception of peace. After having tried it a few thousand times, it may be wise to remember what Francis Bacon said three centuries ago, that "it would be an unsound fancy and self-contradictory to expect that things which have never yet been done can be done *except by means which have never yet been tried.*"

Human society and human evolution, a dynamic phenomenon *par excellence,* can never be mastered by static means.

Treaties are essentially static instruments.

Law is essentially a dynamic instrument.

Wherever we have applied the method of law to regulate human relationship, it has resulted in peace.

Wherever we have applied treaties to regulate human relationship, it has inevitably led to war.

If we continue to refuse to recognize the essence of peace and believe that it is a negative state of affairs which can be "lasting," which can be "kept" for a long time without changes, which can be "enforced" by any means, then the problem of peace will be solved only after we solve the much easier problems of the quadrature of the circle, perpetual motion and how many angels can sit on the head of a pin.

But if we realize that peace is not a *status quo,* that it can never be a negative or a static conception, but that it is a *method,* a method of dealing with human affairs, a method of adapting institutions to the uninterrupted flow of change created by the permanent, inexorable dynamism of life, then the problem of peace is clearly definable and perfectly solvable. Indeed, it has been solved many times in many fields.

Policy, diplomacy, treaties, are static, nation-centric conceptions. The only way to control and canalize dynamic social realities is the proved flexible method of law. Clear recognition of the distinction between the two methods of regulating human relations is of utmost importance in determining the direction we wish to take.

The method of treaties and the method of law are qualitatively different and can never converge. We can never arrive at a legal order by means of treaties. If our goal is a society based on law, then it is imperative to start afresh.

The confusion existing in this field is alarming. Many government officials and political writers, in discussing national sovereignty, argue that every time a nation signs a treaty with another nation and undertakes certain obligations, it surrenders parts of its sovereignty. This is an absolute fallacy. The signing of treaties by national governments, far from limiting or restricting their sovereignty, is the very criterion of national sovereignty.

A strange paradox lies embedded in the dogmatic minds of our statesmen and political thinkers. It is the traditional belief, inherited from the past and entirely dominating their outlook and actions, that there are two different ways of maintaining peace between men.

The one—universally recognized and applied *within* national, sovereign units, is—Law, Order, Government.

The other, so far used *between* sovereign national units, is—Policy, Diplomacy, Treaties.

This is a mental aberration, an utterly warped picture of the problem.

Peace can never be achieved by two such totally contradictory methods for the simple reason that peace is actually identical with one of those two methods.

Peace is law. It is order. It is government.

"Policy" and "diplomacy" not only may lead to war, but cannot fail to do so because they are actually identical with war.

The use of force—the act of compulsion and killing—is irrelevant in defining peace and war. It cannot be the criterion of one or the other because force is inherent in both states of society. The application of force by a government within an established social order does not create war. It strengthens and supports the established legal order, therefore strengthens and supports peace. On the other hand, force used as an instrument of policy and diplomacy between social units without previously established law is *identical* with war.

That peace between sovereign nations can ever be achieved by policy or diplomacy—no matter what policy and what diplomacy—whether or not force is at their disposal, is a mirage.

"Peaceful policy," "peaceful diplomacy," are terms of absolute incompatibility. In the world of reality, the methods of policy and diplomacy between sovereign social units are identical with war and can never be anything else.

Several thousand years of social evolution have crystallized this axiom concerning any human society:

Peace among men can only be achieved by a legal order, by a sovereign source of law, a democratically controlled government with independent executive, legislative and judiciary bodies. A legal order is a plan laid down by the common consent of men to make their individual lives, their families and nations secure. Of all the methods hitherto tried, this alone has proved capable of developing and carrying out changes in human relations without violence.

The other method, the method tried and tried again to keep peace between sovereign units of any type and any size, the method dogmatically and stubbornly adhered to by our national governments, has invariably failed at all times, in all places and under all circumstances. To believe that we can maintain peace among men living in separated, sovereign national units, by the method of diplomacy and policy, without government, without the creation of sovereign lawmaking, independent judiciary and executive institutions expressing the sovereignty of the people and equally binding on all, is a mere dream.

To try to prevent war by the use of policy is like trying to extinguish fire with a flame thrower.

Agreements and treaties between national governments of equal sovereignty can never last because such agreements and treaties are the products of mistrust and fear. Never of principles.

Diplomacy, like military strategy, consists of hoodwinking, tricking and outwitting the other party. In every other field of human activity, if someone succeeds in making his opponent believe the exact opposite of his real intentions we call this man a liar, a deceiver, a cheat. In military life he is regarded as an outstanding tactical genius and becomes a general. In diplomacy, he is looked upon as a great statesman and he is called Your Excellency.

Law is the only foundation upon which social life in modern society can exist. We cannot rely on men's promises not to murder, on their pledges not to steal, on their undertakings not to cheat. That is why we have to have laws and courts and police, with duties and functions clearly defined in advance.

We all recognize that when we talk of individual freedom, we mean a synthesis of freedom and compulsion, as quite obviously freedom is a relative notion which depends not only upon the extent to which we are free to act as we please, but equally upon the extent to which the free actions of others affect us.

It is extraordinary that despite recognition from time immemorial of this elementary and self-evident truth, we still ignore the essence of individual and group interdependence in the relations of nations, in international life.

In international relations we still talk about the "independence" of nations in absolute form, believing that a nation is independent only if it has absolute sovereignty to do whatever it wants, to sign treaties with other sovereign powers and to "decide" upon war and peace. We categorically reject any regulation of that national sovereignty on the ground that this would destroy national independence.

In the past we have tried to regulate the relations of nations on the basis of pledges, promises and treaty obligations. We have seen that this did not work. It is not surprising that such a structure always broke down. The extraordinary thing is that it worked between recurrent wars even for the briefest space.

The old system crumbled because a peaceful collaboration of independent sovereign nations based on mutual treaty obligations is an impossibility—like some acrobatic feat no trapeze artist could perform.

The independence of a nation, just like that of an individual, does not rest solely on its freedom of action, but equally on the degree to which the freedom of action of other nations may infringe upon its own independence. Independence of nations, therefore, does not mean that each nation should be free to choose the form of government it wishes; it means that relations between nations must be regulated by law.

Our task is not to devise a *status quo*—no matter how just—but to proclaim fundamental principles, and on their basis to set in motion machinery for the creation of law.

If world society is again based on treaties, then no change in the established *status quo* is possible without war.

Only if we base international relations on law—just as we base on law the relations of individuals and groups within organized society—can we hope that the constant and inevitable evolution essential to life will be brought about by peaceful methods within that legal order.

The dogma of "national sovereignty," which is supposed to overawe us, has no relevance in this connection. In either case—whether we stay on a treaty basis or set up a legal order—sovereignty is vested in the people. The difference is that in the treaty system sovereignty of the people is not exercised in sufficiently effective form because each sovereign nation-state has power over a limited area only, without any possibility of control over other sovereign nations seeking changes in the existing *status quo;* whereas in a world based on law, changes in international relations could for the first time be carried out without violence—by legally instituted procedure.

Any treaty—the best or the worst—will bring another war. History offers hundreds of instances to bear out this assertion and not a single exception to disprove it.

We cannot prevent crime. For thousands of years we have tried to do so in our social life and we still have murderers and thieves and kidnapers. But what we have been able to achieve is to define quite clearly what we mean by crime, to establish a certain system of laws with coercive force; to establish independent courts to apply these laws and to establish police, prisons and punitive measures to give effect to the decisions of courts of law.

This is the only thing we can realistically hope to achieve in our international life. But this we can achieve if we agree upon the proper diagnosis of this world crisis and if we realize that when we talk about international peace we mean exactly the same thing as when we talk about keeping the peace within a nation—in other words, order based on law.

CHAPTER X

SUPER-STATE AND THE INDIVIDUAL

IN OUR modern industrial world, nation-states are not only the greatest obstacle to world peace. More and more they are the destroyers of the most cherished individual liberties in a democracy.

We have seen:

1. That in all stages of history, social units of equal sovereignty in contact inescapably get into conflict and war.

2. That a phase of human history marked by a series of clashes between a particular type of equal sovereign units comes to a close when sovereign power is transferred from the conflicting groups to a higher unit.

3. That a transitory period of relative peace follows each such transfer of sovereignty.

4. That a new cycle of wars begins as soon as the new units of equal sovereignty come into contact with each other.

These cycles of peace and war in human society through transfers of sovereignty from existing, conflicting social units to higher units, run parallel with the development of individual human freedom.

Whenever, through human effort—evolution or revolution—individual freedom in varying degrees was achieved and granted within existing social units, these liberties flourished only until the social units in which they were established came into contact with other units of equal sovereignty. Once such contacts became effective they inevitably resulted in friction and conflict between the units, and they inevitably led to the limitation, restriction and finally, to the destruction of individual freedom, in the interest of the presumed security and the power of the social unit as a whole.

This development can be observed in the history of primitive tribes, of the Greek and Renaissance city-states, of mighty empires, of world religions, of great economic enterprises and of modern nation-states.

The present trend toward strengthening central government power to the detriment of individual liberty within the modern nation-states is a trend identical with this evolution during many phases of history in all parts of the world. It is a permanent phenomenon in human development. Contacts between social units create competition, arouse jealousies, foster conflicts and lead to violent clashes which, in turn, react by creating a tendency toward centralized power and crushing individual liberty in every sovereign unit within this sphere of contact.

In this era so prodigiously prolific of secret weapons and political slogans, another concept has been launched by the enemies of progress, a concept destined to become the object of passionate debate. This term is: super-state. It sounds terrifying. All men of healthy instincts are supposed to react in unison: We will have none of it!

Any attempt to establish a legal order beyond the boundaries of the present nation-states is to be discredited and defeated by the rhetorical question: "Do you want to live in a super-state?"

What is a super-state? Is a super-state a state of vast dimensions? Or is it a state with an overlarge population? Or is it a too-powerful state?

Since the beginning of thought, writings about the nature and the problems of the state in human society would fill whole libraries. In this century-old search for the truth about the state, two conceptions have crystallized. One is the theory that the state is an end in itself, the purpose of society, the ultimate goal. Individuals have to obey the dictates of the state, submit to the state's rules and laws, with no right of participation in their creation. Without the state the individual cannot even exist. This conception of the state found expression in autocratic kingdoms and empires throughout history. Since the destruction of most of the absolute monarchies, it has returned in our age in the form of Fascism, Nazism, the dictatorship of a single party or military caste.

The other conception of the state—the democratic conception—sees the ultimate goal in the individual. According to the democratic theory of the state, the individual has certain inalienable rights, sovereignty resides in the community, and the State is created by the people who delegate their sovereignty to state institutions for the purpose of protecting them—their lives, their liberties, their properties—and for maintaining law and order within the community.

Our ideal is the democratic state. The state we want to live in is one which can guarantee us maximum individual liberty, maximum freedom of religion, speech, press and assembly; maximum freedom of communication, enjoyment of scientific progress and material wealth. We want the state to restrict and control these individual freedoms only to the extent to which innumerable free individual actions interfere with each other and make necessary regulation of the interdependence of individuals within a society—a legal order. Throughout the whole nineteenth century, such has been the development of the great democratic nations toward greater wealth and more individual freedom.

But this development reached its zenith at the beginning of the twentieth century, when industrial progress began to overflow and undermine the structure of the eighteenth century nation-state. In order to reinforce the structure, in every one of the nation-state units, artificial measures had to be taken on a scale that could only be undertaken by governments. A development started which, in the greater part of the world, led to the complete destruction of all individual liberty.

In some countries like Germany, Italy and Spain, this change was undertaken openly and purposely by suppressing individual liberty, and by proclaiming the principle that salvation lies in the all-powerful totalitarian nation-state endowed with the right to dispose of the very lives of its citizens.

In other countries, like the United States, Great Britain, France, the development has been slow, gradual and against our will. We have continued to uphold democratic ideology but little by little we have given up more and more of our individual liberty to strengthen our respective nation-states. It is immaterial which parties were in power and were instrumental in bringing about these changes. Right and Left, conservative, liberal, socialist, capitalist and Communist forces evolved in the same direction. It is wide of the mark to blame any government or any political party for the growing centralization of state administration. The trend is irresistible. Any other governments or parties in power would have been forced to take the same measures in their struggle against involvement in foreign wars with other nation-states and in their fight against violent social conflicts at home.

Under the double threat of imminent and inescapable war, as pressure from outside, and growing social conflicts, economic crises and unemployment, as pressure from inside, it was and is imperative for each nation to strengthen its state by instituting or expanding military service, by accepting higher and higher taxation, by admitting more and more interference of the state in the everyday life of the individual.

This trend seems the logical result of the present conflict between the body politic and the body economic in our nation-states. In a world which industry and science have transformed into a single huge entity, our political ideologies and superstitions are hindering growth and movement.

Violent conflicts between nations are the inevitable consequence of an ineffective and inadequate organization of relations between the nations, and we shall never be able to escape another and another world war so long as we do not recognize the elementary principles and mechanics of *any* society.

It is a strange paradox that at any suggestion of a world-wide legal order which could guarantee mankind freedom from war for many generations to come, and consequently individual liberty, all the worshipers of the present nation-states snipe: "Super-state!"

The reality is that the present nation-state has become a super-state.

It is this nation-state which today is making serfs of its citizens. It is this state which, to protect its particular vested interests, takes away the earnings of the people and wastes them on munitions in the constant fear of being attacked and destroyed by some other nation-state. It is this state which, by forcing passports and visas upon us, does not allow us to move freely. It is this state, wherever it exists, which by keeping prices high through artificial regulations and tariffs, believing that every state must be economically self-supporting, does not permit its citizens to enjoy the fruits of modern science and technology. It is this state which interferes more and more with our every-day life and tends to prescribe every minute of our existence.

This is the "super-state"!

It is not a future nightmare or a proposal we can freely accept or reject. We are living within it, in the middle of the twentieth century. We are entirely within its orbit, whether in America, in England, in Russia or Argentina, in Portugal or Turkey.

And we shall become more and more subject to this all-powerful super-state if our supreme goal is to maintain the nation-state structure of the world. Under the constant threat of foreign war and under the boiling pressure of economic problems, insolvable on a national basis, we are forced to relinquish our liberties, one after the other, to the nation-state because in final analysis our tribalism, our "in-group drive," our nationalism, is stronger than our love of freedom or our economic self-interest. At the present stage of industrialism, the nation-states can maintain themselves in one way alone: by becoming super-states.

The super-state which we all dread and abhor cannot be qualified by the territory over which it extends or by the number of citizens over which it has authority. The criterion of a super-state can be only the degree to which it interferes with individual liberties, the degree of collective control it imposes on its citizens.

The Italy of Mussolini in 1925 was much more a "super-state" than the United States of Coolidge, although the latter was twenty-five times larger. Tiny Latvia, under the dictatorship of Ulmanis, was much more a "super-state" than the Commonwealth of Australia, covering a whole continent.

We cannot have democracy in a world of interdependent, sovereign nation-states, because democracy means the sovereignty of the people. The nation-state structure strangulates and exterminates the sovereignty of the people, that sovereignty which, instead of being vested in institutions of the community, is vested in sixty or seventy separate sets of sovereign nation-state institutions.

In such a system, the sovereignty of each group tends to cancel out the sovereignty of the others, as no institution of any one group can ever be sovereign enough to protect its people against the infringements and dangers emanating from the fifty-nine or sixty-nine different sets of institutions in the other sovereign groups.

Absolute national sovereignty, as incarnated by our national governments, could operate satisfactorily only in a condition of complete isolation. Once a situation exists in which several sovereign nation-states are in contact with each other, their inevitably growing interdependence, their ever-closer relations completely modify the picture. In a world of sixty or seventy sovereign nation-states, the real sovereign power of a nation to determine—independently from influences radiating from other sovereign nation-states—its own course and its own actions is reduced to a minimum. The tendency within such an interdependent system is to reduce to zero, to cancel completely and to annul any real sovereignty or self-determination of the conflicting national units.

At the present stage of industrial development, there can be no freedom under the system of sovereign nation-states. This system is in conflict with fundamental democratic principles and jeopardizes all our cherished individual freedoms.

As the sovereign nation-states cannot prevent war, and as war is becoming an indescribable calamity of ever-longer duration, we are periodically called upon to sacrifice everything for sheer survival.

We cannot say that our individual freedom is guaranteed if every twenty years all our families are torn apart and we are forced to go forth to kill or be killed.

We cannot say that our welfare and economic freedom are guaranteed when every twenty years we have to stop production of consumer goods and waste all our energies and resources in the manufacture of the tools of war.

We cannot say that we have freedom of speech and the press when every twenty years conditions force censorship upon us.

We cannot say that private property is guaranteed if every twenty years gigantic public debts and inflation destroy our savings.

Defenders of national sovereignty will argue that all these restrictions and suppressions of individual liberty are emergency measures, necessitated by the exigencies of war and cannot be regarded as normal.

Of course, they are emergency measures. But as the nation-state structure, far from being able to prevent war, is the only and ultimate cause of the recurrent international wars, and as the aftermath of each of these international wars is simultaneously the prelude to the next violent clash between the nations, eighty or ninety per cent of our lives are spent in times of "emergency." Under existing conditions, periods of emergency are the "normal" and not the "abnormal."

If we want to stick to the obsolete conception of nation-states, which cannot prevent wars, we shall have to pay for worshiping this false goddess with the sacrifice of all our individual liberties, for the protection of which, ironically, the sovereign nation-states were created.

World wars such as have been twice inflicted on this generation cause such major catastrophes, are so horribly costly in human life and material wealth that before all else we must solve this central problem and establish freedom from fear. It is a foregone conclusion that unless we do this we cannot have and shall not have any of the other freedoms. Within a nation-state, as within a cage, freedom of action, individual aspirations, become a mockery.

It is all the important to recognize the primordial necessity of a universal, political and legal order because there is not the slightest possibility that we can solve any one of our economic or social problems in a world divided into scores of hermetically sealed national compartments. The interrelationship and interdependence of the nations are so evident and so compelling that whatever happens in one country immediately and directly affects the internal life of all the other countries.

It is pathetic to watch the great laboring masses of common men aspire to better conditions, higher wages, better education, more leisure, better housing, more medical care and social security, while they struggle under the most appalling conditions. There can be no question that these are the real problems of the overwhelming majority of men and women and it is perfectly comprehensible that the ambitions and desires of hundreds of millions are focused on these issues.

Yet, the very fact that these problems are everywhere regarded as national matters, problems which can be solved by national governments through national institutions, makes these aspirations unattainable dreams. In themselves, they are within the reach of reality. Scientific and technological progress have brought them to our very door. For a fraction of the time, money, thought and labor wasted on international wars, social and economic conditions could be transformed beyond recognition. But under the certain threat of recurrent wars, all these social aspirations of the people are being indefinitely postponed. Even if in one country or other legislation to this effect is enacted, it will be crushed and buried by the next global war, like mountain huts by an avalanche.

Full employment within the compartmented political structure of sovereign nation-states is either a myth or Fascism. Economic life can develop on a scale to provide work and goods for all only within a world order in which the permanent threat of war between sovereign nation-states is eliminated, and the incentive to strengthen the nation-states provided by the constant fear of being attacked and destroyed is replaced by the security that a legal order alone creates.

Social and economic problems are essentially problems of a Copernican world, insolvable with nation-centric, Ptolemaic means.

National leaders seriously declare in one breath that we must maintain untrammeled national sovereignty, but that we must have free trade between the nations.

Free trade without free migration is an economic absurdity, a mathematical impossibility.

But the nation-states, like feudal knights, are chaining their subjects to the soil of their homeland, refusing them that most elementary of freedoms, the freedom of movement. The interference of the nation-states in this field of human liberty is identical with the absolute rule of the feudal landowners over their serfs. The system of passports, visas, exit permits, immigration quotas, is incompatible with free economic exchange.

Were it possible to assign to nations the economic roles they must play, like casting a theatrical production, the problem of international trade would be simple. If Spain could be persuaded to concentrate on growing oranges, Brazil on producing coffee, the Argentine on raising beef, France on manufacturing luxuries, Great Britain on weaving textiles and the United States on making automobiles, it would be relatively easy to persuade people of the advantages of a free and unhampered exchange of products between the nation-states.

But the economic roles thus allotted to the nations are not equally important or equally profitable from a political point of view, and therefore each national unit naturally tends to produce everything possible at home. There is not the slightest chance that the United States will ever stop producing grain and meat so that Canada and the Argentine may freely export their grain and meat products to the United States. Nor will Great Britain and France ever agree to stop building ships and motorcars so that United States shipyards and industrial plants may freely sell their products all over the world.

Once a certain number of closed national units are in existence, each producing a certain amount of almost every commodity, and once each sovereign nation is dominated by the idea of strengthening its national economic machinery, freedom of exchange between these units becomes impossible without the stronger producer nation dominating the weaker. Free trade between such divided national economies would inevitably cause shutdowns in a great number of industries in many of the countries and would make it impossible for several countries, working under less favorable conditions, to sell their agricultural products.

Such a calamity—brought about by the sudden abolition of tariff walls between the sovereign nation-states—could be remedied only if the masses, as they became unemployed in certain parts of the world, were free to migrate to those places where the freedom of competition resulting from the abolition of tariffs, would create prosperity and new opportunities for employment and investment in specific fields.

If the nations maintained the existing restrictions on migration, abolition of protective tariffs would bring about conditions in many nations which no sovereign nation-state could nor indeed ever would accept and sanction.

The Malthusian superstition regarding immigration that exists in all the nations of the world is so strong today that it is impossible to imagine the sovereign nation-states easing their rigid policies aimed at prohibiting immigration.

The fallacy that immigration above all creates pressure on the labor market, lower wages and unemployment is so deep-rooted; the failure of the still underpopulated new countries to realize that, on the contrary, wealth is created by man is so striking, that freedom of migration between sovereign nation-states is politically unrealizable. Without it, freedom of trade between sovereign nation-states is unimaginable.

Free trade cannot function *between* sovereign units. To have free trade between larger territories, we must first eliminate the obstacle of political frontiers dividing the peoples.

Another *conditio sine qua non* of a free world economy—which alone can produce under present-day conditions enough wealth to secure economic freedom—is a stable currency. It is a truism that a well-functioning, highly rationalized and integrated economy requires a stable standard of exchange. But this elementary problem has never been satisfactorily solved and can never be solved within the political nation-state framework.

Without a stable and generally accepted standard, no national economy could have developed as it actually did. And no further progress in international economy is thinkable without a universally accepted, stable standard of exchange.

Every few years, the entire system of international trade gets out of gear because of some difficulty in the peculiarly constructed world monetary system. Currency is a jealously guarded attribute of national sovereignty and each nation-state insists upon having its own national currency and determining its value as it pleases, by internal, national, sovereign decision.

So it is a terrible and constantly recurring problem how to "stabilize" the exchange rates between the United States and France, between England and Spain, between each and any of the national sovereign economic units.

But it is no problem at all to keep the currency

in permanent relationship between Michigan and South Carolina, between Cornwall and Oxfordshire. The reason is very simple. One single currency is in circulation.

Economists and statesmen say that such a solution could never be applied between nations because their living standards are not on the same level and rich countries would suffer from any monetary union. This economic commonplace hardly stands examination. The difference in wealth between nations is no greater than the difference in living standards between the South Carolina tobacco farmers and the Detroit industrialists in the United States, the Breton fishermen and the Parisians in France, or between rich and poor regions to be found inside any nation.

The fact is that, just as unified national currency was necessary to facilitate the development of national economies up to their present level, so a unified world currency is the indispensable condition for further development of world economy from the present stage on.

"International monetary agreements," "stabilization funds," "international banks," "international clearing houses," "international barter arrangements" can never create stability of exchange rates. If we maintain scores of different national currencies, each an instrument of sovereign national policy, no amount of banking acrobatics can ever keep them balanced, as each sovereign nation will at all times regard its own national economic interests as more important than the necessity of international monetary stability.

The complicated machinery of world economy, world-wide production, world-wide use of raw materials, distribution on the world markets, demands a stable standard of exchange that only a single world currency can provide. As long as it is the sovereign attribute of sixty or seventy social units to cheat each other by selling a hundred yards of cloth in exchange for fifty pairs of shoes and then, by a national sovereign decision, to reduce the length of the yard from three feet to two feet, there is no hope for freedom in world economic exchange.

No matter how it hurts our most cherished dogmas, we have to realize that in our industrialized world, the greatest threat to individual liberty is the ever-growing power of the national super-state.

As a direct result of national sovereignty, we are living today in the worst kind of dependency and slavery.

The rights of the individual and human liberty, won at such a cost at the end of the eighteenth century through the overthrow of personal absolutism, are more or less lost again. They are on the way to being completely lost to the new tyrant, the nation-state.

The fight for liberty—if it is liberty we want—will have to be fought anew, from the very beginning. But this time it will be infinitely harder than it was two centuries ago. Now we have to destroy, not men and families but tremendously strong, mechanized, sacrosanct, totalitarian institutions.

Those who will fight for the lost freedom of man will be persecuted by the nation-states more ruthlessly and cruelly than were our forefathers by the absolute monarchs.

PART THREE

CHAPTER XI

FALLACY OF INTERNATIONALISM

NONE of the dominant conceptions of political thought is more abused, more discredited, more prostituted, than "internationalism."

Internationalism is such a useless word. It is disliked by the great majority of peoples and compromised by its association with the Catholic church, socialism, big business, Communism, Jewry, cartels, Freemasonry, Fascism, pacifism, armament industry and other movements and organizations opposed one and all by the majority of the human race. Also it is an utterly misleading term.

It may prove a blessing that internationalism has been compromised in so many aspects. From its inception, internationalism has been an entirely erroneous notion. It has retarded political and social progress by half a century.

Rather early in the industrial age, people of various classes and professions within the various nation-states began to feel restrained and hindered by their national barriers. Efforts were made to try to overcome these barriers, by establishing contacts and working out common programs, common movements, common organizations between groups with similar interests in different countries. For a certain time these organizations no doubt strengthened the position and influence of those who took part in them. But far from overcoming the difficulties which induced their creation, such international organizations stabilized and perpetuated the conditions responsible for the difficulties.

Internationalism means exactly what it says. It expresses: *Inter-Nationalism.*

It does not and never has opposed nationalism and the evil effects of the nation-state structure. It merely tries to alleviate particular symptoms of our sick world without treating the disease itself. Paradox it may be—but nothing has added more to the strength of national institutions, nothing has fanned nationalism more than internationalism.

The founders of modern socialism assumed that the working classes—ruthlessly exploited, as they believed, by the capitalist states—could feel no loyalty toward their particular nations. The interests of the laboring masses in every country were thought to lie in opposing and combating capitalist states. Consequently, the proletariat was organized on an international basis, in the belief that the loyalty and allegiance of the workers would be the exclusive appanage of the internationally organized Socialist party.

But neither the First nor the Second nor the Third Internationale saw that allegiance and loyalty to a nation-state has little, if anything, to do with the economic and social position of the individuals in that state. They made no attempt to weaken or destroy the nation-state as such. Their aim was to overthrow the capitalist class and transfer political power to the proletariat within each nation-state. They thought that such independent, heterogeneous national revolutions taking place in many countries through coordinated action, either simultaneously or following each other, would solve the social problem, abolish war between nations, create world peace.

It was soon obvious that these "international" working class organizations changed nothing in the world-wide trend toward nationalism. All working organs of the Internationales were composed of "delegates" from all the various nations, from socialist parties whose task was to defend the interests of their own national groups and among whom serious differences of opinion existed at all times. The moment organized socialist workers in the various countries had to choose between loyalty to their comrades in the internationally organized class warfare within nations, and loyalty to their compatriots in the nationally organized warfare between nations, they invariably chose the latter. Never in any country did organized labor withdraw its support from the nation-state in waging war against another nation-state, even though the latter had a laboring class with the same resentments, the same ideals and the same aims as its own.

Through a fundamental contradiction in its program, modern socialism is particularly to blame for strengthening nationalism and for the inevitable consequence: international war. The contradiction lies in the discrepancy between the socialist political ideal of internationalism and the socialist economic ideal of nationalization of the means of production.

It is difficult to understand how, during an entire century, and particularly in the face of the events of the first part of the twentieth century, not one of the socialist or Communist leaders called the attention of his followers to the fact that nationalization of the land and of industries cannot be reconciled with the political ideal they call "internationalism."

The greater the extent of nationalization, the more power is vested in the nation-state, the more impregnable becomes nationalism. The stronger the nation-states, the more inevitable and the more imminent is the danger of conflict between them. The coexistence of three score and ten odd sovereign nation-states with all economic power in the hands of each nation-state is unthinkable without frequent and violent conflicts. Wars between nations—or the threat of such wars—lead to restrictions of individual rights, to longer working hours, lower living standards, freezing of wages, outlawing of strikes, reduction of consumption, conscription, regimentation—in short, to everything labor is supposed to be fighting.

The socialist and Communist parties must realize that through their program of "nationalization" they have done more to strengthen and buttress the modern totalitarian nation-states than have the aristocracy or any feudal or capitalist ruling class. This tragedy is the result of acting emotionally on first impulses, without thinking the problem through. The workers of the world must realize that through their misconception and through their self-deluding ideal of internationalism, they are preventing the realization of their ideals of peace and betterment of economic and social conditions.

By advocating nationalization, the socialists originally had in mind, of course, collectivization, the transfer of certain property rights from individuals to the community. During the first half of the nineteenth century, the concept of the nation was almost identical with the ideal of the community, and the confusion of the two at that time is understandable. But at the present stage of industrial development, in the middle of the twentieth century, nothing is more remote from the ideal of the community than the nations. They have shrunk into tightly sealed compartments obstructing any community expression. From the point of view of the community, national and private interests differ scarcely at all. Both are particular interests.

"Nationalization" today no longer means collectivism but its opposite. Human collectivity, at the present stage of evolution, is without institutions and consequently without reality.

If socialists and Communists believe that tools and means of production or indeed anything, should belong to the community, they must first give reality to the ideal of community before the transfer of any kind of authority to that community can have meaning. Confusing the nation-state with the community is a most dangerous error, as today nation-states are the mortal enemies of the ideal of human community, far more than any landowner, industrialist or private corporation.

The same misconception prevails among socialists as to economic planning. They believe that the present anarchic conditions of production guided exclusively by the profit motive can be remedied by economic planning. They would have production guided not by motives of immediate profit, but by the long-range needs of the consuming masses.

That for smoother and more efficient functioning the economic process in its present stage needs a certain amount of guidance and directives emanating from authorities higher than the individual manufacturers, can no longer be disputed if we understand the laws regulating all social activities, including economic activity. But the realization of this necessity is an altogether different thing from the assertion that national governments should control such economic planning.

In theory, it is conceivable that the economic life of each nation might be controlled and planned as minutely as possible by government authorities. But if such planning is regarded as a national problem; if all plans and regulations are undertaken by national governments, applicable only to their own national populations; and if there are seventy-odd independent systems of planning devised by the sovereign nation-states in their own particular interest, the result can only be confusion, clash of interests, conflict, war—the exact opposite of planning.

In the middle of the twentieth century, we see that industrial workers, organized in socialist and Communist parties, are the most intransigent nationalists, the stanchest supporters of their respective nation-states. Without even mentioning Soviet Russia, where identification of the Communist party with the Soviet state explains to some extent the nationalist fervor of Soviet labor, the organized industrial workers in the United States, Great Britain, France and other democratic countries represent forces demanding higher and higher tariff barriers; restriction if not prevention of immigration; racial discrimination and a series of measures that are clearly reactionary, in which they go hand in hand with their national governments. In any relationship between national units, they totally disregard the interests of their fellow workers living in other nation-states.

Internationalism among the capitalist forces was exactly similar in its development.

Industrialists, bankers, traders, also began to feel hampered by the barriers of nation-states and began to form organizations reaching beyond national boundaries. By and large, they succeeded in arriving at agreements which excluded competition in their respective domestic markets, in fixing minimum prices and in regulating competition on the world market.

Most of these measures were naturally detrimental to consumers the world over. But their greatest drawback was that they failed to solve satisfactorily or for any length of time the problems they were supposed to solve. Far from leading to a reconciliation of divergent national interests, such international financial and cartel agreements served only to intensify nationalism among industrialists and bankers, all anxious to strengthen their own positions as national units, against other national units.

The national contingents of these international producing and financing corporate bodies became completely identified with the interests of their nation-state and in every country governments were backing them by economic policies designed to strengthen the national representatives in these international economic organizations. The direct results of these attempts to internationalize big business led to an acceleration of economic nationalism, higher tariffs, irrational subsidies, currency manipulations, and all the other devices of government control repugnant to the principles of free enterprise.

All these attempts by private interests and political forces to overcome the obstacles arising from the rigid framework of the nation-states were utterly futile.

After the ravages of the first World War, the representatives of the nation-states, the national governments themselves, felt that something had to be done to bridge the constantly widening abyss between nations, and to prevent a repetition of such devastating wars between them.

From this necessity, the Covenant of the League of Nations was born, drafted mainly by Woodrow Wilson, Colonel House, Lord Cecil and Léon Bourgeois. According to the Covenant, peace was supposed to be maintained through regular meetings and discussions of representatives of sovereign nation-states having equal rights in an Assembly of all nations and in a Council, comprised of representatives of the great powers, as permanent members, and a limited number of smaller powers elected as temporary members by the Assembly. No decision was possible over the veto of any nation. Unanimity was necessary to apply any effective measure. Any national government could withdraw from the League the moment it did not like the atmosphere.

The spirit of the Covenant was as irreproachable as the bylaws of an exclusive London club, open to gentlemen only. But it was somewhat remote from reality. The League had some success in non-political fields. It did excellent research work, and even settled minor political clashes between small nations. But never in its entire history was the League able to settle a conflict in which one of the major powers was involved. After a few short years, the construction began to totter and crack. When Japan, Germany and Italy withdrew, it was obvious that the political value of the League of Nations, its ability to maintain peace between the nations, was equal to zero.

It is useless to argue what would have happened *if...*

If the United States had joined the League...If Great Britain and the U.S.A. had sent their navies into Japanese waters in 1931...If France, England and other European powers had marched into Germany when Hitler repudiated the Locarno Pact and occupied the Rhineland...If Britain and France had closed the Suez Canal and had used force to prevent Italian aggression in Ethiopia...If the members of the League had gone to the defense of Austrian independence...And many more 'if's'...

The historical fact remains that never on any occasion was the League of Nations capable of acting when action would have involved the use of force against any of the leading military powers. To say that this was not the fault of the League, that it was the fault of the powers who would not support the League, makes no sense. The League was, after all, nothing more than the aggregate of the nations that composed it.

The League of Nations failed because it was based on the false notion of *inter-nationalism,* on the idea that peace between national units, between sovereign nation-states, can be maintained merely by bringing their representatives together to debate their differences, without making fundamental changes in their relations to each other.

Since the foundation of the League of Nations, events have moved with fatal rapidity into the second phase of the twentieth century world catastrophe, which occurred on September 1, 1939, exactly as if the League had not existed. It is not too much to assume that the rhythm of this series of inexorable events was even accelerated by the existence of the League, because the frequent meetings of representatives of the sovereign nation-states served only to intensify their mutual distrust and suspicion.

Besides the functioning of the League, between the two world wars we have witnessed innumerable international conferences, composed of the representatives of national governments, on political, military and economic matters. All of them failed, although for a short time one or two of them gave the illusion of success. But even these exceptions, widely publicized as successes, were nothing more than pious expressions of vague and unreal hope, like the Kellogg Pact that was certainly not worth the traveling expenses of the national delegates.

In spite of these experiences, in spite of the immeasurable misery and suffering of this universal catastrophe caused by the clash of national units, our governments and political parties, supported by the vast majority of a misled, gullible and unenlightened public, have nothing better to offer than a repetition of what has been proved and proved again a total fallacy: peace and the prevention of war by treaty arrangements between sovereign nation-states.

With the one sole exception—when in a moment of despair in June, 1940, Winston Churchill suggested union between Great Britain and France—all the utterances and declarations of our governments and political leaders of all parties demonstrate that they are incapable or unwilling to contemplate anything except such an *international* organization.

All the political manifestations during World War II—the Atlantic Charter, the United Nations declaration, the Moscow agreements, the Dumbarton Oaks proposals, the Teheran and Yalta communiqués, the San Francisco Charter—underline, specify and emphasize that whatever may be done is to be done and will be done between sovereign nation-states.

The world outlook expressed by the word "internationalism" embodies the greatest misconception and the gravest error of our generation.

Inevitably it will continue to fortify the nation-state structure, at a time in history when our only salvation and chance to progress lies in weakening and finally destroying that framework. Any artificial setup to overcome difficulties by "bringing together," by "mutual understanding between" the delegates of nation-states is not only bound to fail but will unnecessarily prolong the agony of our obsolete, moribund political system.

To realize clearly the implications of internationalism, we must bear in mind the meaning of nationalism.

In this our day and generation, nationalism dominates democracy, socialism, liberalism, Christianity, capitalism, Fascism, politics, religion, economics, monarchies and republics. Nationalism is the soda water that mixes with all the other drinks and makes them sparkle.

Nationalism is a herd instinct. It is one of many manifestations of that tribal instinct which is one of the deepest and most constant characteristics of man as a social creature. It is a collective inferiority complex, that gives comforting reactions to individual fear, loneliness, weakness, inability, insecurity, helplessness, seeking refuge in exaggerated consciousness and pride of belonging to a certain group of people.

This urge, today called nationalism, has been virulent at all times and in every civilization, manifesting itself in many different ways. The origin and quality of this transcendental mass emotion are probably unchangeable, but the object toward which it directs itself has undergone manifold and radical transformations throughout history. In the long evolution of human society, the "in-group drive" was transferred from the family to the tribe, village, city, province, religion, dynasty—up to the modern nations.

The object is always different. But the emotional herd instinct itself remains the same. And it constantly causes conflict between the various units until the object of the "in-group drive" is integrated into a larger, broader group.

According to the democratic conception, the nation is the totality of the population living within one state bound together by common ideals. The nation is, therefore, an elastic concept. During the past centuries, it has constantly changed and grown and the allegiance of peoples has changed and grown with it.

People from Massachusetts and people from Georgia did not feel the same "nationalism" in 1850 that they feel today. Englishmen and Scotsmen owed allegiance to different states and symbols before 1707. So changed the "nationalism" of the Piedmontese and the Tuscans, the Burgundians and the Gascons. The Uzbeks were not always Russian nationalists and the Saxons did not always fight side by side with the Prussians.

Nationalism, like any other group emotion, can be directed toward a different object without changing the quality or intensity of the emotion. But at no time in history and upon no occasion was it possible to reconcile and to maintain peace between distinct and conflicting groups of men driven by the same emotions.

Inter-nationalism countenances nationalism.

It implies that the various nationalisms can be bridged. It recognizes as supreme the sovereign nation-state institutions and prevents the integration of peoples into a supra-national society.

We have played long enough with the toy of internationalism. The problem we are facing is not a problem between nationalisms. It is the problem of a crisis in human society caused by nationalism, and which consequently nationalism or internationalism can never solve.

What is needed is—universalism. A creed and a movement clearly proclaiming that its purpose is to create peace by a legal order between men beyond and above the existing nation-state structure.

CHAPTER XII

FALLACY OF SELF-DETERMINATION OF NATIONS

DURING the second World War, Wilson has often been blamed for a series of grave errors of procedure, for not handling the situation properly after the first World War. Others, defending Wilson, say that the League of Nations failed, not because of any mistake Wilson made, but because the nations composing the League did not live up to the obligations they assumed.

Those who criticize Wilson's actions say that he made a great mistake in not taking a representative committee of American Senators with him to the peace conference in Paris. Had leading members of the Foreign Relations Committee of the United States Senate participated in the negotiations preceding the Versailles Treaty, the Senate would have ratified the Covenant. Had America become a member of the League, the argument continues, the second World War would never have broken out.

By taking to Paris a delegation with only one Republican, who was neither a Senator nor prominent in the party, Wilson offended the Senate and the Republican party, with the result that the treaty was not ratified. To avoid a repetition of that tragedy, this time representatives of both parties in the Senate should participate in drafting the new world organization.

Wilson is also blamed for having insisted upon the inclusion of the Covenant of the League in the Treaty of Versailles. So the conclusion was drawn that this time we should set up the world organization separately from the peace arrangements.

Wilson insisted on the equality of nations, members of the League. As that principle did not work, we are now to have a league dominated by the great powers, who actually *are* responsible for keeping the peace.

Wilson insisted that the coalition created by the war, the Allied and Associated Powers, be dissolved after the cessation of hostilities and that the new League take over the settlement of all further problems and disputes, including the application of the peace treaties. That method having failed, the grand alliance created by the war is to be maintained and the proposed world organization to have nothing to do with the peace settlement or with the conditions imposed upon the defeated enemy countries.

Wilson insisted upon general disarmament. As that program proved ineffective to maintain peace, this time the great powers are to remain armed to prevent any further aggression and protect the peace.

Wilson insisted on immediate settlement after the cessation of hostilities. Now we are to postpone political, territorial and economic decisions and make special transitional arrangements before we discuss "final" settlements.

Thus goes the dispute. Arguments and more arguments are adduced, blaming the failure of Wilson on the opposition of "bad men," on the secret treaties of the Allies, on the mistake he made by going to Europe personally, on the fact that he took principles and no plans to Paris, on his stubbornness in dealing with the Senate between February 14 and March 13, 1919, when he was back in Washington, and so forth.

All these arguments criticizing Wilson's acts and policies are entirely superficial. None of them even approaches the core of the problem.

Having reversed our policy and applied methods and procedures the exact opposite of Wilson's methods and procedures, without changing the fundamentals of our approach to the problem, the result will be exactly the same.

Granted that the new covenant for a world league was almost unanimously accepted by the United States Senate; now if we made a just peace with the enemies of the United Nations; if we maintained the grand alliance to enforce the post-war settlements; if we created a world organization of all "peace-loving" nations with the United States and the U.S.S.R. participating; if the great military powers maintained heavy armaments to prevent "aggressions"; if the great powers were charged by the proposed world organization to maintain and enforce peace with their armed might—in brief, if we followed a procedure diametrically opposed to the procedure of 1919, the result would be the same: another world war in a short time.

We shall never learn the lessons of the swift and complete collapse of the 1919 world order, if we confine ourselves to formal and superficial discussions of method and policy.

Less wide of the mark, though altogether fallacious, is the view that the League and the world order of 1919 crumbled, not because of any errors committed in 1919 nor because of any weakness of the League, but because the nations refused to fulfill their Covenant and failed to act at critical moments as they had promised and were supposed to act.

So at the end of the second World War, we find statesmen asserting that the 1919 world structure failed because the ideals and principles of Wilson were abandoned. According to them, there was nothing whatever wrong with the underlying principles upon which that order was erected.

The historic fact is that the second World War came about, not because Wilson's doctrines were not carried out, but because they were!

If we wish to avert further disappointments and another major catastrophe, we must try to understand the essential errors and fundamental fallacies of Wilson's ideas.

Although there are a few indications that Wilson did aim at the establishment of a "sovereignty of mankind," his ideas as laid down in the Fourteen Points, Four Principles, Four Ends, Five Particulars and finally in the Covenant of the League, all point most distinctly in an opposite direction.

The basic thought of Wilson was that every nation and every people is entitled to self-government, political independence and self-determination and that a league of independent and sovereign nations should guarantee the independence and sovereignty of each and every nation.

In the eighteenth century this would have been a feasible conception. But in the twentieth century such an oversimplified and superficial solution was bound to lead to total anarchy in international relations. This conception clearly demonstrates that Wilson, his associates in the creation of the 1919 world order and all the millions who today seek solutions along the same lines, are unable to clarify the confusion in their minds as to elementary social and political principles.

Self-determination of the nations is a Ptolemaic conception.

Self-determination is an anachronism. It asserts the sacred right of every nation to do as it pleases within its own frontiers, no matter how monstrous or how harmful to the rest of the world. It asserts that every aggregation of peoples has a sacred right to split itself into smaller and ever smaller units, each sovereign in its own corner. It assumes that the extension of economic or political influence through ever-larger units along centralized interdependent lines is, in itself, unjust.

Because this ideal once held good—in a larger, simpler, less integrated world—it has a terrific emotional appeal. It can be used and is being used by more and more politicians, writers, agitators, in slogans calling for the "end of imperialism," the "abolition of the colonial system," "independence" for this and that racial or territorial group.

The present world chaos did not come upon us because this or that nation had not yet achieved total political independence. It will not be relieved in the slightest by creating more sovereign units or by dismembering interdependent aggregations like the British Empire that have shown a capacity for economic and political advancement. On the contrary, the disease now ravaging our globe would be intensified, since it is in large measure the direct result of the myth of total political independence in a world of total economic and social interdependence.

If the world is to be made a tolerable place to live in, if we are to obtain surcease from war, we must forget our emotional attachment to the eighteenth century ideal of absolute nationalism. Under modern conditions it can only breed want, fear, war and slavery.

The truth is that the passion for national independence is a leftover from a dead past. This passion has destroyed the freedom of many nations. No period in history saw the organization of so many independent states as that following the war of 1919. Within two decades nationalism has devoured its children—all those new nations were conquered and enslaved, along with a lot of old nations. It was, let us hope, the last desperate expression of an ideal made obsolete by new conditions, the last catastrophic attempt to squeeze the world into a political pattern that had lost its relevance.

Quite certainly, independence is a deep-rooted political ideal of every group of men, be it family, religion, association or nation.

If there were only one single nation on earth, the independence of its people could very well be achieved by its right to self-determination, by its right to choose the form of government and the social and economic order it desired, by its right to absolute sovereignty.

Such absolute national self-determination might still guarantee independence if in all the world there were only two or three self-sufficient nations, separated from each other by wide spaces, having no close political, economic or cultural contact with each other.

But once there are *many* nations whose territories are cheek by jowl, who have extensive cultural and religious ties and interdependent economic systems, who are in permanent relations by the exchange of goods, services and persons, then the ideal of self-determination—of each nation having the absolute right to choose the form of government, the economic and social systems it wishes, of each having the right to untrammeled national sovereignty—becomes a totally different proposition.

The behavior of each self-determined national unit is no longer the exclusive concern of the inhabitants of that unit. It becomes equally the concern of the inhabitants of other units. What the sovereign state of one self-determined nation may consider to the interest and welfare of its own people, may be detrimental to the interests and welfare of other nations. Whatever counter-measures the other self-determined sovereign nations may take to defend the interests of their respective nationals, equally affect the peoples of all other national sovereign units.

This interplay of action and reaction of the various sovereign states completely defeats the purpose for which the sovereign nation-states were created, if that purpose was to safeguard the freedom, independence and self-determination of their peoples.

They are no longer sovereign in their decisions and courses of action. To a very large extent they are obliged to act the way they do by circumstances existing in other sovereign units, and are unable to protect and guarantee the independence of their populations.

Innumerable examples can be cited to prove that, although maintaining the fiction of independence and sovereignty, no present-day nation-state is independent and sovereign in its decisions. Instead, each has become the shuttlecock of decisions and actions taken by other nation-states.

The United States of America, so unwilling to yield one iota of its national sovereignty, categorically refusing to grant the right to any world organization to interfere with the sovereign privilege of Congress to decide upon war and peace, was in 1941 forced into war by a decision made exclusively by the Imperial War Council in Tokyo. To insist that the declaration of war by Congress following the attack on Pearl Harbor was a "sovereign act" is the most näive kind of hairsplitting.

Nor was the entrance of the Soviet Union into the second World War decided by the sovereign authorities of the U.S.S.R. War was forced upon the Soviet Union by a sovereign decision made in Berlin.

The failure of national sovereignty to express self-determination and independence is just as great in the economic field, where every new production method, every new tariff system, every new monetary measure, compels other nation-states to take countermeasures which it would be childish to describe as sovereign acts on the part of the seventy-odd sovereign, self-determined nation-states.

The problem, far from being new and insoluble, is as old as life itself.

Families are entirely free to do many things they want to do. They can cook what they like. They can furnish their home as they please. They can educate their children as they see fit. But in a Christian country no man can marry three women at the same time, no man living in an apartment house can set fire to his dwelling, keep a giant crocodile as a pet or hide a murderer in his flat. If a person does these or similar things, he is arrested and punished.

Is he a free man or is he not?

Clearly, he is absolutely free to do everything he wants in all matters which concern himself and his family alone. But he is not free to interfere with the freedom and safety of others. His freedom of action is not absolute. It is limited by law. Some things he can do only according to established regulations, others he is forbidden to do altogether.

The problems created by the ideal of self-determination of nations are exactly the same as the problems created by the freedom of individuals or families. Each nation can and should remain entirely free to do just as it pleases in local and cultural affairs, or in matters where their actions are of purely local and internal consequence and can have no effect upon the freedom of others. But self-determination of a nation in military matters, in the fields of economic and foreign affairs, where the behavior of each nation immediately and directly influences the freedom and safety of all the other nations, creates a situation in which self-determination is neutralized and destroyed.

There is nothing wrong with the ideal of self-determination.

But there is something very wrong indeed with the ideal of "self-determination of nations."

This concept means that the population of this small world is to be divided into eighty or a hundred artificial units, based on such arbitrary and irrational criteria as race, nationality, historical antecedents, etc. This concept would have us believe that the democratic ideal of self-determination can be guaranteed and safeguarded by granting people the right of self-determination within their national groups, without giving corporate expression of self-determination to the aggregate of the groups.

Such a system can preserve self-determination of the people only so long as their national units can live an isolated life. Since the nations today *are* in contact, with their economic and political lives closely interwoven, their independence needs higher forms of expression, stronger institutions for defense. In absolute interpretation, the many self-determined national units cancel out each other's self-determination.

What was the use of the "self-determination of Lithuania" when self-determined Poland occupied Vilna? And what was the use of "Polish self-determination" when self-determined Germany destroyed Poland? Unquestionably, self-determination of nations does not guarantee freedom and independence to a people, because it has no power to prevent the effects of actions committed by *other* self-determined nations. If we regard the freedom and self-determination of peoples as our ideal, we must do our utmost to avoid repeating the mistakes of 1919 and realize that *"self-determination of nations"* is today the insurmountable obstacle to *"self-determination of the people."*

Nobody realized the dangers of the predominating forces of our age better and sooner than

Winston Churchill. In an article, published in the United States in February, 1930, he wrote:

"The Treaty of Versailles represents the apotheosis of nationalism. The slogan of self-determination has been carried into practical effect. The Treaties of Versailles and Trianon, whatever their faults, were deliberately designed to be a consummation of that national feeling which grew out of the ruins of despotism, whether benevolent or otherwise, just as despotism grew out of the ruins of feudalism. All the inherent life thirst of liberalism in this sphere has been given full play. Europe is organized as it never was before, upon a purely nationalistic basis. But what are the results? Nationalism throughout Europe for all its unconquerable explosive force, has already found and will find its victorious realization at once unsatisfying and uncomfortable. More than any other world movement, it is fated to find victory bitter. It is a religion whose field of proselytizing is strictly limited and when it has conquered its own narrow world, it is debarred, if it has no larger aim, by its own dogmas from seeking new worlds to conquer."

And, after a brilliant analysis of the fallacy of a world order based on absolute national sovereignty, and on the ideal of national self-determination, Churchill concluded, in 1930:

"No one can suppose that this is going to last."

It did not last. But the emotional hold of these eighteenth century nationalist ideals are all-powerful in the minds of our national statesmen.

A decade later, the same Winston Churchill, as Prime Minister and the unforgettable and unchallenged leader of the democratic forces against totalitarianism, proclaimed the very same principles of consummated nationalism and self-determination as the foundation upon which the coming world order was once again to be built—the very principles which ten years before he so correctly recognized as futile and their victory unsatisfying and bitter.

The aggregation of acts in every possible combination and permutation—the product of the self-determination of all sovereign nation-states—creates an inextricable network of effects and counter-effects, within which the ideal of independence becomes ridiculous.

In a small interrelated and interdependent world, it is obvious that the ideals of independence and self-determination are relative notions. Independence and self-determination can exist in fact only as an optimum, can be achieved only through the regulation of the interrelations of the self-determined sovereign units.

The Polish people would have been independent and would have had self-determination to a much higher degree than was actually assured them by the sovereign Polish Republic, had certain attributes of Polish national sovereignty been limited, restricted and integrated into a higher sovereign institution, provided that the sovereignty of the German state had been equally limited, restricted and integrated. The first criterion of independence and self-determination is the ability to guarantee freedom against aggression and destruction by outside forces. Today the institutions of the sovereign nation-state are patently incapable of fulfilling that task.

The Covenant of the League of Nations was based entirely on the principles of national sovereignty, of national self-determination, on the right of every nation to do as it pleased within the boundaries of its national state. The Covenant was built upon the assumption that peace between such sovereign nation-states could be maintained by providing a place for the representatives of these sovereign units to meet and discuss their relationship, and the machinery to handle the problems arising between them.

This was a purely formal and unrealistic conception which did not even recognize the existence of the crucial problem of human society that must be solved, the evident and apparent causes that lead to conflicts and to wars between the nations. With such complete lack of understanding of the nature of international conflicts, with such basically erroneous notions as to the essence of group relationship, Wilsonism and its creation, the League, was bound to fail, no matter what policies, what procedure, what tactics, were pursued by its founders, no matter what attitudes were adopted by its member states.

CHAPTER XIII

FALLACY OF COLLECTIVE SECURITY

F OR some thousands of years we have been struggling for peace. That we have never reached our goal does not prove that peace is unattainable. But it does prove that the means and methods by which we have tried to achieve it are inadequate.

In 1919, completely misunderstanding the forces of his time and the meaning of the crisis which he was called upon to solve, Woodrow Wilson rejuvenated all the eighteenth century conceptions of nationalism. The order created after the first World War was the apotheosis of nationalism, of national sovereignty, of self-determination of nations, of the right of each nationality to its own sovereign state.

For twenty years the world agonized in the strait-jacket of this rigid structure which prevented organic integration of the nations, led to higher and higher tariffs, to mistrust, unemployment, hatred, misery, dictatorships, armaments and—the second World War.

It would seem that all these horrible events might have shaken the blind confidence in those outdated and deadly dogmas, and that the people who have to lead the nations through this holocaust might at least have searched for the real causes of the crisis and for the path that could lead us out of it.

The tragic fact, however, is that we are neither heading nor thinking in a new direction. Those in power have no time and no incentive to think. And those who think have no power whatsoever.

All the documents and pronouncements of the governments of the United Nations prove that they have nothing else in mind than a return to the old policies that failed so completely. It is a strangely topsy-turvy world in which all governments, statesmen, diplomats, politicians and party leaders are ardent protagonists of theories and conceptions so evidently at variance with the realities of our time.

During the second World War the documents in which are crystallized the thoughts of the United Nations are the Atlantic Charter, the United Nations Declaration, the Moscow, Teheran and Yalta agreements, the Dumbarton Oaks proposals and the San Francisco Charter.

When the Atlantic Charter was first proclaimed, the democratic world was thrilled to the marrow. That thrill derived more from the event itself than from the contents of the proclamation. After a series of Brenner Pass meetings between Hitler and Mussolini, each the prelude to further Axis triumphs, the high-seas meeting between Roosevelt and Churchill was novel and dramatic; it held the promise of triumphs for the enemies of the Axis.

Does the Atlantic Charter—does the world view implicit in that document—offer a new approach to the solution of international problems?

The underlying idea of the Atlantic Charter is expressed in its third paragraph: "They (the President of the United States and the British Prime Minister) respect the right of all peoples to choose the form of government under which they will live; and they wish to see sovereign rights and self-government restored to those who have been forcibly deprived of them."

That is the charter of the first World War.

That is a reiteration of the old doctrine of self-determination, upon which we built the world of 1919 that crumbled so miserably and so quickly. The Atlantic Charter again proclaimed the right of every nation to choose the form of government it desires—or the form imposed upon it by a ruthless minority. It bowed abjectly before the fetish of "national sovereignty" with all that it implies: unlimited terror and organization for aggression within any nation so inclined; nonintervention in military epidemics until too late; blind isolationism and neutrality in a world made small by science and interdependent by industry.

The Atlantic Charter, for all its fine intentions, is an anachronism. If applied it would divide the world into more and yet more nations, each of them independent of the others, unlimited in its sovereign right to do mischief. It recognized the right of any country to be as undemocratic and to-talitarian as it pleases, a law unto itself. It failed to recognize and to implement larger sovereignties that transcend national sovereignties, human rights that take precedence over national rights.

Self-determination is no guarantee of independence. The sad fate of the small nations set up at Versailles proves that. Even before their freedom was finally wiped out by the rampant and self-determined nationalism of Nazi Germany, they could maintain the illusion of independence only by accepting the patronage and protection of one of the more powerful nations. Independence in its absolute form produces only fear, mistrust, conflict, slavery—because it penalizes pacific nations and gives the right of way to aggressors and troublemakers among countries.

The third paragraph of the Atlantic Charter, in one terse phrase, enshrines the tragic misunderstanding of our generation.

We all assume it to be true that freedom and independence are the inalienable rights of man, and we are seeking to create institutions to guarantee and safeguard those rights. In the eighteenth century our forebears found those guarantees and safeguards in the principle of national sovereignty, in the institutions of the sovereign nation-state, controlled by the people, and in the rights of all peoples to self-determination, to choose the form of government, the structure of their political and economic system within the territorial boundaries of their state, to do so of their own free will without foreign interference.

These concepts and these institutions, in their absolute form, were perfectly capable of expressing and protecting national independence as long as contact between the established national units was either nonexistent, unnecessary or loose. Since modern industrialism, science and communications have shrunk this planet of ours into a sixty-hour flying trip, and will continue to shrink it further; since no nation, not even the mightiest, is economically self-sufficient; since industry seeks to gain markets all over the world and can develop only within a framework where exchange and free communication are possible, these eighteenth century concepts, as expressed in the treaties of 1919 and in the Atlantic Charter, create in their absolute form, conditions similar to a society in which individuals may act as they please, without any limitations on their impulses, without any consideration as to the effect of their actions on other members of that society. In their absolute form, the principles upon which the Atlantic Charter is based lead straight to anarchy in international life.

If this present trend cannot be reversed, we are heading toward nationalism more frenzied and delirious than ever. If we cling to the principle of self-determination of nations, we shall have to face the claims of the innumerable nationalities in Europe, Asia, even in Africa, to have sovereign states of their own.

The principle of "self-determination of nations" is a primitive and oversimplified expression of the concept of national independence. It is designed to work in laboratory conditions. Present-day realities, however, produce too many interferences to make possible the application of such a hypothetical formula without recurrent explosions.

The right of one man is the fruit of the obligations of all men. In social life, this is self-evident. No organized society is conceivable without a codification of the rights and duties of all members of that society. Now, irresistible and inexorable events force us to organize the relations of nations. In international life, however, we refuse to acknowledge this fundamental principle of society, and insist that a workable world order be built upon a Bill of Rights without a Bill of Duties. We fail to recognize that what made the Bill of Rights and the Declaration of the Rights of Man possible were the Ten Commandments.

The Atlantic Charter, far from explaining the causes of this world catastrophe and indicating the road to real freedom and independence, again lured mankind toward the mirage of peace, toward a belief that we can have peace and all our cherished democratic ideals if only we give every nation complete self-determination and "the right to choose its own form of government."

The ideals of group independence and group self-determination have degenerated into an idol which must be destroyed in our minds if we ever want to see again exactly what that ideal really means.

In the Atlantic Charter as well as in all the other documents and pronouncements relating to a future world organization, there lies an implication that is a dangerous fallacy. This is the widespread and generally accepted notion about the nature and causes of aggression.

Aggression is popularly considered the root of all international evils, the cause of all wars. This fundamentally erroneous premise logically leads to the equally erroneous conclusion that the task of peacemakers is to suppress aggression.

The idea of setting up inter-national machinery with no other purpose than to "prevent aggression" —to "keep the peace"—as the slogan goes, not only misses the point completely, but indeed may become the source of grave consequences.

Peace is conceivable only as a social order having the machinery necessary to carry out all the organic changes and modifications in human society that may at any time be required by the natural and uninterrupted development of that society.

Such an order of never-ending reform is the only alternative to recurrent outbreaks of violence. This only known alternative is the Rule of Law.

If there were no national legal order, then violence between the individuals, religions, parties, classes and other groups within a given nation would be inevitable. Violence under such conditions is an absolutely natural phenomenon, indispensable, unavoidable, even desirable for carrying out changes required by permanently evolving human society.

We know that so long as we believe in peace between sovereign nations and endeavor to maintain an established *status quo* between these nations (no matter what *status quo*) we shall have wars. If, on top of this policy, which failed as often as it was tried in the past, we are going to create an international "security organization" to "prevent aggressions" or to stamp out aggression by force when it does occur, then we shall have created, certainly not peace but higher pressure on a society that is simmering, stronger obstacles to the irresistible torrent of events, which are bound to cause more and more violent eruptions, because in such an order change without violence is exceptional, if not impossible.

To condemn aggression irrespective of the conditions within which it takes place is a superficial truism which can never solve a problem of such complexity. We can never have peace and security by aiming at negative, static conceptions, like "preventing aggressions." If we want to live a more civilized life, we shall simply have to go through the painful labor of setting up "a standard to which the wise and the honest can repair," proclaiming principles and fighting for them.

At one time, there were seven Saxon kingdoms in England eternally waging wars against each other. Then a foreigner, a conqueror from Normandy, crossed the Channel, invaded the island and unified the bickering, quarreling, warring Saxon tribes. By no imaginable moral standard was this a justifiable act in the eyes of those who lived on the island. It was clearly a case of brutal, unprovoked aggression. But was it evil? Was the unification of the English kingdoms, although brought about by a foreign conqueror, wrong?

The conquest of the American West was unquestionably another case of brutal, unprovoked aggression. But was this opening of the American continent, this unification by aggressive methods, evil?

The planners of future peace should beware of their fundamental illusion: that they can create an order to last forever. No one can put this world into a strait-jacket. No one can design an order and freeze it into permanent shape. It is against the nature of things to create a system of national boundaries and alliances, of economic organization, and then command history to stand still; to consider anyone who attempts to change this order an "aggressor."

When the essence of life is perpetual change, adherence to worn-out forms and static conceptions must lead to explosions, wars and revolutions. Static structures, too weak and rigid to withstand the storms of events, will be blown away like a house of cards.

Here is the fundamental fallacy of the idea of collective security, based on treaty agreements between sovereign nations, which seems to be the one and only dogma upon which this generation can visualize a world order.

All the peace treaties ever signed, all the alliances ever concluded on this planet, the Covenant of the League of Nations, the United Nations Organization, the principles of collective security, are *identical* in their fundamental conception.

They all arbitrarily divide the world into a number of sovereign social units, create a *status quo,* and try to prevent any changes in the established order except by unanimous consent, which makes no sense; or by force, which makes war.

The Covenant of the League, the Dumbarton Oaks and San Francisco documents, the notion of collective security, are all static, Ptolemaic conceptions. They are antidynamic and consequently represent only barriers to peace, to life itself. They all seek solutions on a basis which—if it existed— would leave no problems to be solved.

Collective security without collective sovereignty is meaningless. The insecurity of the individual as well as of groups of individuals is the direct result of the nonexistence of law to govern their relations. Allowing sovereign sources of law to reside, not in the community but in the eighty-odd separate nation-states forming that community; attempting to make their coexistence peaceful, not by establishing institutions with sovereign power to create law binding all members of the collectivity but by agreements and treaties between the divided sovereign units, can never, under any condition, create security for that collectivity. Only a legal order can bring security. Consequently, without constitutional institutions to express the sovereignty of the community and to create law for the collectivity, there can be no security for that collectivity.

The debate among the representatives of the

nations in drafting the charter of a world organization was exclusively limited to formalities and
technicalities which have absolutely no bearing
upon peace and the future of mankind. All the representatives of national governments are in full
agreement in rejecting the only foundation upon
which a peaceful international order could be
constructed.

One of the technicalities is the question of voting
within a council of sovereign nations. According to
the Covenant of the League, in case of an "aggression" by any sovereign member state of the
League, sanctions could be taken only by unanimous consent. Naturally, this made the functioning of the inadequate League machinery—which
under no conditions could have prevented major
wars—utterly illusory.

No sovereign nation-state will ever freely admit
that it is an aggressor, nor of its own free will, will
it submit to sanctions imposed by other sovereign
nations. So whenever a nation was accused by the
League of aggression or threatened with sanctions,
it merely tendered its resignation and left the
party.

The accusing nations behaved just as hypo-
critically. When the consequences of such collective action were to be faced and decisions carried
out against the offending nations, all the other
sovereign members of the League followed the
private interests of their individual nation-states.
The use of force against any major power was
unthinkable. That meant war.

This tragi-comic game will be repeated again and again, so long as we believe that a league or a council of sovereign nation-states can, under any circumstances, maintain peace among its members.

In a society without any system of law, no individual would ever trust a judge, a jury or a court, even if composed of the most eminent and selfless of his fellows. No individual would ever freely submit his personal freedom and fortunes to the judgment of any group of men composed of members with no higher authority than his own. No individual would ever submit of his free will, without defending himself by all means at his disposal, to interference in his life by a force, if the actions of that force had not previously been delineated and defined.

Individual members of a society are prepared to submit to one thing alone. To Law. They are ready to submit to social institutions only insofar as those institutions are the instruments of Law.

Such law is nonexistent in our inter-national life. It never did exist in inter-national relations. It has been excluded from the League of Nations and from the United Nations Organization. Under these circumstances, there can be no peace between nations.

To base "peace" on unanimous decisions of a certain number of sovereign national governments—in the present day, on the unanimous decisions of the five greatest military powers—means indulging in a daydream. It is an Alice-in-

Wonderland adventure. And in seriously proposing such an organization and assuring the peoples of the earth that the five greatest military powers will—by common consent and unanimous decision—act in concert, our present leaders, our governments and diplomats are guilty of monstrous hypocrisy or else of näiveté far greater even than Alice showed in her adventures in dreamland.

History proves beyond doubt that any real danger to world peace always emanates from one of the major military powers. It is to be expected that in every situation threatening the existing order, one of the major powers will be seriously involved. It is clear that the major power will not cast its vote in any inter-national council against its own interests. Consequently, in no major crisis will unanimous vote in the security council be obtainable. Whenever such conflicts arise, as they are bound to arise, the only course open to the others will be to close their eyes and let the events of Manchuria, Austria, Ethiopia, Spain and Czechoslovakia repeat themselves—or go to war.

But even if the nations be prepared to accept majority decisions within such a world council, the problem would remain unsolved. Majority decisions in a council of sovereign nations would be wholly unrealistic. If in a given situation, three of the major powers voted for a certain military intervention, while the other two voted against such a measure, these two powers could scarcely be pictured taking up arms and undertaking military action contrary to what they regard as their own national interests, and contrary to their votes.

So the whole debate on unanimous vote versus majority vote on issues arising in a security council of a world organization is irrelevant because in neither case could a decision on an issue involving a great power be enforced without precipitating a major war.

The conclusion to be drawn is this: The fundamental problem of regulating the relations between great powers without the permanent danger of major wars cannot be solved so long as absolute sovereign power continues to reside in the nation-states. Unless their sovereign institutions are integrated into higher institutions expressing directly the sovereignty of the community, unless the relations of their peoples are regulated by law, violent conflicts between national units are inevitable. This is not prophecy, not even an opinion, but an observable and irrefutable axiom of human society.

Just as a council of delegates and representatives of fifty sovereign cities, defending the interests of their respective municipalities, could never create a united nation, a national legal order, peaceful relations between the citizens of the fifty cities, security and freedom of the individuals living within each sovereign municipality—so the representatives and delegates of fifty sovereign nations meeting in a council and defending their own national interests, will never arrive at a satisfactory solution and settlement of any problem concerning the interrelations of the sovereign national units.

Just as peace, freedom and equality of the citizens of a nation require within their state specific institutions and authorities separate from and standing above municipal or local authorities, and the direct delegation of sovereign power by the people to these higher, national, government authorities—so peace, freedom and equality of men on this earth, between the nation-states, require specific institutions, authorities separate from and standing above national authorities, as well as the direct delegation of sovereign power by the people to these higher world government authorities, to deal with those problems of human relations that reach beyond the national state structure.

None of the projects and plans of a world organization even considers a direct relationship between the "international" organization and the individual. In all these proposed and debated structures, the determining factor continues unchanged to be the nation-state.

All power, all decision, all action, all source of law, continues to rest with national governments. The individual remains the serf of the nation-states. The proposed society as contemplated by our governments, is clearly a society of the modern feudal lords, the nation-states, who are desperately trying to preserve their accumulated and abused privileges and power to the detriment of the peoples they oppress.

In the major countries, particularly in the

United States, people are heatedly debating whether their representatives in the proposed world security council should have power to act of their own volition regarding the application of force in case of an international conflict or whether they should refer back to their governments or to their legislative bodies for final approval.

The underlying point of the controversy against those who would not yield one iota of the rights and privileges of inherited institutions is that if the representative of the United States or of any other country in the world council is not empowered to use armed force against a nation declared to be an aggressor, but is obliged to wait upon the deliberations of his government or legislative body at home, weeks or months may be lost and this delay may paralyze the international machinery. But if the delegates do have full power to order the armed contingent of their countries to enter into action against an aggressor, then the international organization will be strong enough to enforce peace.

This issue is seriously debated by members of governments, by legislators, editors, columnists and radio commentators, as being the crucial issue on which war or peace in the future depends.

It is at once apparent that the controversy is of the shallowest, that the alternative put before us is purely formal. Whether we resolve to take this course or the other, whether the representatives of the five great powers in the security council are empowered to engage the armed forces of their countries in action or whether before such decisions the situation must be debated in Congress or Parliament makes absolutely no difference. The course of events will not be changed by any of the suggested procedures, because the fundamental problem of war and peace has no relationship whatsoever to these procedures.

Whether the application of force is an act of war or a police action depends upon one single criterion: whether or not the force is being used to execute the judgment of a court, applying established law in a concrete case.

If force is used without previously enacted law, defining clearly the principles of human conduct and the norms determining such conduct, then the use of force is arbitrary, an act of violence, war—whether the decision to resort to it be made by a national representative as a member of an inter-national council, by a national legislative assembly, or even by national referendum.

In the charter of the new world organization, there is no provision for the creation of law regulating the relations of the nations. On the contrary, it is clearly stated that sovereign power to create law is the exclusive appanage of the individual nation-states, and that the international organization is an association of such sovereign nation-states.

There being no law to define human conduct in inter-national relations, any use of force is arbitrary, unjustified, an act of war. Such an international organization may succeed in unimportant issues when force can be used by a major power or by a combination of powers against a weak and small nation. It is bound to fail whenever such use of force has to be resorted to by one power or group of powers against another power or group of powers with equal or approximately equal military strength. The application of force against a great power by a small nation in case the great power commits the aggression is, *ab ovo,* unthinkable and need not be discussed.

Such a state of affairs has absolutely nothing to do with the functioning of a police force in society. Such an organization as was the League and as the new international organization drafted at Dumbarton Oaks and San Francisco does not differ in any except external and formal aspects from the state of affairs that has always and at all times existed, without a league or any world organization.

Sovereign source of law remains scattered in *many* units. This always meant and, by the very force of things must always mean, violent conflict between these sovereign units, no matter what their relations, as long as sovereign power continues to reside in each separate unit.

Peace between the conflicting units is possible only if their relations are regulated by a higher sovereign authority embracing all of them. Once this is recognized, once developments are under way for the creation of law in international relations, then the use of force follows automatically, since real law implies its application by force.

But without previously enacted laws for international conduct, any proposal to use force is immoral and dangerous in the highest degree. It is an unforgivably false conception to believe that force without the pre-existence of law can maintain peace and prevent war, if the decision as to its application rests in the individual sovereign nation-states forming the inter-national society, no matter which department of the sovereign nation-states may be endowed with that power.

The tremendous volume of irresponsible talk on this most delicate problem has warped the judgment even of the most illustrious leaders of the United Nations.

In a speech made on October 21, 1944, President Roosevelt, warmly advocating the Dumbarton Oaks agreements, made the following statement:

"The council of the United Nations must have the power to act quickly and decisively to keep the peace by force if necessary. I live in a small town. I always think in small town terms. But this goes in small towns everywhere. A policeman would not be a very effective policeman if, when he saw a felon break into a house, he had to go to the Town Hall and call a town meeting to issue a warrant before the felon could be arrested. It is clear that, if the world organization is to have any reality at all, our American representative must be endowed in advance by the people themselves, by constitutional means through their representatives in Congress with authority to act."

To compare the role of a policeman in a small town with the use of force as suggested by the Dumbarton Oaks documents reveals a complete misunderstanding of the fundamental principles involved. The policeman in a small town is endowed with the power to arrest a felon by previously promulgated laws created by the sovereign legislative body of the society he serves. He is the instrument of a legal order and acts under authority of established law.

The "police force" suggested by the Dumbarton Oaks proposals is not the executive organ of a society having an established legal order based on the sovereignty of that society, but the armed contingents of the sovereign nation-states, the sovereign units composing a society, which itself remains completely without sovereign authority. The Dumbarton Oaks proposals do not contain any suggestions for the creation of law standing above and binding together the individual members of the international society. They do not propose international courts to apply laws, nor could these hypothetical courts function, lacking the laws to apply. And they do not propose police forces to execute such judgments, responsible to the society itself, nor could such hypothetical force be a police force without courts to render judgment according to law.

In a world society organized on the basis of the Dumbarton Oaks proposals, it may well be that the man to do the arresting would be not the policeman but the felon himself.

This is precisely the problem.

The police force, as conceived at Dumbarton Oaks, is no different from the legions of the Roman Empire or the armies of the Holy Alliance. They would be armed forces of sovereign powers or power groups and instruments of particular interests.

To revive the old League of Nations or to create a United Nations council on a similar basis (composed of representatives of sovereign nation-states), is an extremely simple proposition, although many people become emotional in debating the role of great powers and small powers in such a council.

The "idealists" plead for equality between great powers and small nations in the world organization, the "realists" want to give a preponderant role to the great powers, who under any circumstances would have to assume responsibility for checking aggression.

The realists who welcome the resurrection of the League of Nations under another name, with dentures in it (they say "with teeth") arrive at the peculiar conclusion that since no great power would accept military action against itself without resistance, the use of force is practicable only against small nations.

So what they really say is that the use of force against a small nation can preserve peace, but force could not be applied against a great power because that would provoke war.

According to them, the use of force against a

small nation is qualitatively different from the use of force against a great power because in the first instance force brings peace, whereas in the second it brings war.

The hair-raising hypocrisy of mankind is truly astonishing. What this theory amounts to is that the theft of a loaf of bread by a poor man is an illegal act to be prosecuted, but the fraud of a millionaire banker must remain beyond the authority of law.

The assertion that the use of force against a small nation is "police power" whereas the same coercion against a great nation is not "police power" but war, is mere abracadabra. It is the result of muddled thinking, of ignorance of the meaning of the words and terms employed. It is not an attempt to shape policy according to principles; it is an attempt to justify an immoral and intolerable policy by elevating it to the level of a principle.

Force is police power when it is used to carry out the law, whether directed against a small or a great power, whether against a weak, miserable vagrant sleeping on a park bench or a strong, organized gang armed with guns who can shoot back at the police.

And force is *not* police power when it is not used to carry out law—even if it is applied by the unanimous consent of all the powers of the world against the smallest and weakest.

This great power versus small power controversy may go on forever, as it has all the characteristics of a meaningless issue that can be endlessly debated by an avalanche of words hiding particular interests and subjective feelings.

From the moral point of view, it is hard indeed to choose between great powers and small nations.

All great powers behave like gangsters. And all small nations behave like prostitutes.

They must. Under present conditions (not unlike those of the wild West), each great power mistrusts the others, must be permanently armed, keep his gun loaded and within easy reach to shoot it out with the others, if he wants to survive and keep his position. And the smaller powers who have no guns and who would never dare shoot it out with one of the big fellows, must go with those who promise them most, and in return for this protection, do whatever is demanded of them.

In the face of these realities, an organization of such sovereign nations, whether on an equal or an unequal footing, could never prevent another war. It is idealism raised to the nth degree of näiveté to believe otherwise. Such a council of sovereign units could prevent another war only if it could change human nature and make it act and react differently from the way it has been acting and reacting throughout the ages.

The national interests of the powers, large and small, do not run parallel, just as the selfish interests of individuals do not run parallel. If we want to remain on a sovereign nation-state basis, then the only chance of a somewhat longer period without war is to keep the sovereign nation-states as far apart as possible, to reduce contact between them to a minimum and not to bring them together in one organization where the conflict of their interests will only be intensified.

Such superficial formalities have been debated for several decades now, the world running around in circles like a dog chasing its own tail, without even a glimpse of reality. The era of parchment treaties signed by the representatives of "peace-loving nations" or "high contracting powers" is gone, like the age of powdered wigs.

As long as our purpose is to establish peace between sovereign nations, it is wholly irrelevant whether the sovereign national governments maintain relations by the exchange of ambassadors, by dispatching notes to each other via short-wave or pigeon post, or by sending representatives to meet in an assembly or around a council table, with representatives of other equally sovereign nations. These are merely differences in method and procedure. None of them even touches the core of the problem created by the interdependence of a given number of social groups with equal, sovereign attributes.

It seems that the first and last maxim of national governments in quest of peace is "All measures—short of law." As peace is identical with law, it is not difficult to realize why we are no nearer our goal than we have been for centuries.

It is a mysterious characteristic of human nature that we are prepared to spend anything, to sacrifice everything, to give all we have and are when we wage war, and that we are never prepared to take more than an "initial step," make more than a "first beginning," adopt more than "minimum measures," when we seek to organize peace. When will our religions, our poets and our national leaders give up the lie that death is more heroic than life?

The events of the first half of the twentieth century and all the national, political, ideological and economic forces at work today make it inexcusable for us to continue to delude ourselves, to continue to listen to false prophets, no matter how good their intentions, who preach that we may have peace merely by patching up outworn systems and revising archaic doctrines that have always led and will continue to lead to war.

When events and realities conflict with established principles, we must not always think that such events and realities are in "violation" of the principles. Often, the established principles are as false as Ptolemy's astronomical principles and can be rectified only by giving up quixotic ideas and adapting principles to realities as did Copernicus.

CHAPTER XIV

THE MELEE

"THE mob has no ruler more potent than superstition."

Observing the human race running amok against their own interests today, exposing their own families, their own cities, their own people and their own countries to destruction, one must sadly admit the correctness of these words of Curtius.

No ultramodern composer could produce shriller dissonance, more chaotic atonality, greater cacophony, than the public discussion raging on the surface of the real problem.

This debate upon the future world order presents nothing but credulity and sterility on one side and on the other nothing but destructiveness and sterility.

Credulity is not faith.

Destructive criticism brings neither revolution nor progress.

Let us examine some of the more popular arguments raised against the rule of law among the peoples.

In any democratic world organization having power to create law, China would have three times as many representatives as the United States, India ten times as many as Great Britain,

Russia five times as many as France. Would the United States, Great Britain, France and the other smaller democratic countries be willing to enter into such a scheme?

Population figures are held up, like a scarecrow, to frighten us away from our objective.

No Chinese or Indian ever sought representation in any international organization on the basis of population.

This very question was hotly debated whenever and wherever representative government was established. In the United States of America, although the population of the state of New York is 122 times larger than that of Nevada, they both send two Senators to Washington. Even in the House of Representatives, the state of New York elects only forty-five times as many representatives as Nevada, a third of what it should, according to population figures. It is natural that in any universal organization created today, representation should be determined by actual responsibilities and according to effective power, industrial potential, degree of education. Various proved methods exist and can be applied to work out this purely technical question.

The very raising of this question shows how little the problem is understood. Under the present system of absolute national sovereignty 130 million Americans, 45 million Britons and not quite 40 million Frenchmen are each faced with about two billion other peoples, whose actions and policies they cannot control or influence in any crisis anyway, except by means of war.

Under a system of universal law, within a universal legal order, America, Great Britain, France and every other individual nation would, for the first time in history, have legal power to influence the actions of other nations constituting more than ninety per cent of mankind and could have a voice in shaping the behavior of other peoples in their own best interests—without war.

There is not the slightest danger that, in a world of realities, within a legal order, China with her numerical superiority in population could outvote the Unites States of America, as long as the real power relationship between the two countries is as it prevails today. But, at some future date, should China become industrialized to an equal extent with America, should China be able to produce three times more consumer goods, build up and maintain a mechanized army, navy and air force three times greater than the United States, then naturally and under any circumstances, power and influence would shift automatically from the United States to China.

If a universal legal order is functioning when such an eventuality occurs, then the change will take place peacefully, without violence, by legal adjustments, by shifting of votes and influence. If there is no universal legal order, then a China three times more powerful will attack, defeat and conquer the United States.

Realities can never be circumvented by sleight of hand. Our choice in adapting our society to existing and changing realities is merely between law and violence. We never have a choice between change and immobility.

Another objection is that should an international police force be established entirely independently of the nation-states and under the sole authority of a world government body, it would have to be larger than the armed forces of any one nation-state. Would the United States, would the Soviet Union, would Great Britain be willing to see an international armed force greater than their own?

This question also misses the point. In the past and present scheme of things, the combined armed forces of the other nations—those of the Soviet Union, Great Britain, France, Germany, Italy, Japan, etc.—were always considerably larger than the armed forces of the United States. The totality of armed forces of all the nations has always been unquestionably greater than those of any independent sovereign nation. And sovereign nations have had absolutely no control over this overwhelming military superiority of the other nations.

Only through the establishment of a universal force to maintain law and order and to prevent violence between nations, would the United States, the Soviet Union, Great Britain and any other country, for the first time in history have direct authority over the armed forces of other nations, be in a position to exert influence over them and have a voice in their use.

Objections of this sort to the creation of an

international legal order are endless. They all run along the same line. All are based on the misconception of national sovereignty, holding to the misguided notion that by establishing a universal legal order we *give up* something instead of creating something. They are blind to the fact that it is under the existing system of absolute national sovereignty that the peoples are living under a sword of Damocles, subjected to dire dangers against which they seek effective and permanent protection.

Few people feel that they have "surrendered" their freedom in allowing the policeman on the street corner to carry the gun. Of course, in the jungle or on the American frontier a hundred years ago, nobody could safely have given up his gun. But life without a gun in a society having a legal order is infinitely more secure than life with any number of guns in a society without a legal order.

Many people assert that any world-wide social organization is bound to fail because nations are fundamentally disinterested in other nations and are unwilling to participate in other peoples' affairs. This superficial idea lies at the roots of any policy of neutrality or isolationism.

Isolationism is a most natural impulse. Every individual, every family, every nation, once having reached a certain position, a certain degree of satisfaction, wants to "be left alone" and "not to be disturbed" by strangers or outsiders. This natural drive is the root of conservatism. It has existed at all times in all powerful countries and in all wealthy classes. It is not a national but a social characteristic. It exists in every country, wherever men live together in groups.

The grandparents of the most stubborn isolationists of Missouri and Wisconsin were pioneers, explorers, adventurers, who went out into foreign lands, exterminated the native inhabitants, took possession of their lands and settled there. If ever in human history there was an act of unprovoked aggression, of unlawful intervention it was the American conquest of the West. Three generations later, the descendants of these expansionists and interventionists have become conservative isolationists.

There is nothing wrong with isolationism. But there is something very wrong indeed with what today is called the "isolationist policy": the policy of Lodge, Borah, Johnson and Wheeler, who thought that the American people could live a secure isolated life through what they called "isolationist policy." They presumed that America could mind its own business, be left alone and might pursue the American way of life, if only the Federal government of the United States maintained its untrammeled national sovereignty and if the sovereign Federal government kept away from any foreign entanglement and commitment.

Within the span of a single generation, two world wars into which the United States has been dragged against the will of its people prove conclusively the bankruptcy of such a policy. It also proves the failure of "splendid isolation" in England and of neutrality in Holland, Belgium and many other countries.

The reasons are apparent. Where can an individual live an isolated life? Certainly not in physical isolation in a tropical jungle. There he has to be on guard day and night to preserve his life and to fight beasts and savages ready to prey on him. A man can live an isolated life much more easily in a civilized city where his security is guaranteed, where there is a legal order, where laws, courts and police watch over his physical existence and individual rights.

Quite certainly no nation can safely live its own isolated life in the jungle of the present world. The alternative is not "isolation" or "intervention in the affairs of other nations." If this were the case, and if nonintervention in foreign affairs could protect people from foreign wars, then isolationalism would unquestionably be the soundest policy. But the alternative is a different one. It is "isolationism" or "the prevention of intervention by other nations in one's own affairs."

For instance, it seems elementary that the first condition to safeguard the rights of the American people to live their own way of life, is security against foreign attack, the certainty that German submarines cannot sink American ships and that Japan cannot attack American territories by surprise.

The policy advocated by the exponents of isolationism and neutrality is the policy least apt to achieve such security from foreign aggression or intervention. Only a constitutional organization regulating the relations between nations by law and strong enough to protect the nations against foreign attacks would permit the people to "be left alone," to "mind their own business" and to pursue their own way of life, as is desired not only by isolationists but by the overwhelming majority of all peoples.

Perhaps long-range robot bombs and radio-propelled heavy bombers will open the eyes of those who have always made their political principles dependent on geographic distance.

Certain people are fearful of broadening the powers of government, asking whom we could possibly trust to decide upon issues so vast and vital. Such fears are very well founded indeed. Upon careful examination of our contemporaries, it does seem that there is no one to whom we could blindly entrust any important public office.

If people in the late eighteenth century could have discussed the vast powers embodied today in the office of the President of the United States of America or that of the Prime Minister of Great Britain, they would probably have decided that such offices should not be created, as no man would be trustworthy or able to hold them. But we have learned that the question of leaders is of secondary importance. In a well-organized and smoothly functioning democratic society, where the duties and responsibilities of offices are clearly defined, a great number of men capable of serving as high officials are always available. There is no need to worry about who would be members of a world parliament, a world court or a world executive. Once the proper, democratically controlled machinery is established, we can safely resort to the old-fashioned method of electing ordinary, fallible, mortal men to office.

Any political system in which the fate of the people depends upon the wisdom or shortsightedness of leaders is fundamentally wrong. Great statesmen are so rare, and among the few born such an infinitesimal number ever get to power, that we cannot rely upon leaders of genius. We must resign ourselves to being governed by mediocre men. Our salvation lies not in the wisdom of leaders but in the wisdom of laws.

But how are the suggested transformations in the political construction of the world possible, when the loyalty and allegiance of all peoples go entirely to their nation, their country, their national flag? How in 1940 could Winston Churchill have stopped the tide of Nazi conquest and aroused the English people without appealing to their national pride—their loyalty to king and country?

Certainly he could not have done it. But neither would it have been possible for Adolf Hitler to have aroused the German people and to have driven them toward brutal aggression and conquest without appealing to their national pride and loyalty to their Reich and flag.

Nationalism undoubtedly helped to defend

England and to inspire the heroic underground resistance against German conquest in France, Poland, Norway and other Nazi-occupied countries. But these beneficial effects of nationalism are similar to the effect of an antitoxin. Because the diphtheria bacillus is necessary to prepare the serum to fight diphtheria, this does not justify calling the virus itself beneficial or useful. At the present stage of bacteriology, the best we can do to cure diphtheria is to use its virus for the preparation of an antitoxin. But it would be much better to destroy and exterminate the causes of diphtheria, even if, at the same time, we destroyed the agent to cure the disease.

Many times in history we have seen how easy it is to change allegiances and loyalties. Within a few short years, a mixture of every nationality in the world created the American nation and, in the second World War, the grandchildren of German immigrants have been the leading military commanders of the United States armies against Germany.

We cannot expect loyalty to an institution that does not exist. The institution must be created before we can demand loyalty to it.

There is no reason to doubt that once universal institutions are established which bring people security, peace, wealth, which unite them in common ideals and common interests, the loyalty of the peoples, today claimed by the inefficient institution of the nation-state, will infallibly turn to them.

Real patriotism, real love of one's own country, has no relationship whatsoever to the fetishism of the sovereign nation-states. Real patriotism can have but one single purpose: to protect one's own country, one's own people, from the devastation of war. As war is the direct result of the nation-state structure, and as modern aerial and mechanized warfare indiscriminately destroys women, children, cities and farms, the nation-state is Enemy No. 1 of patriotism.

Once larger units are established as sovereign social units, there is no reason why nationalism, in its original conception of patriotism, could not and should not continue to flourish. Real patriotism actually needs the protection of law. As soon as people realize that in fact the nation-state institution destroys their countries, devastates their provinces and murders their kinsmen, true patriots will revolt against that institution, a threat to everything they love. Nothing is more incompatible with true patriotism than the present nation-state structure of the world and its inevitable consequences.

"If, in despotic statecraft, the supreme and essential mastery be to hoodwink the subjects, and to mask the fear, which keeps them down, with the specious garb of religion, so that men may fight as bravely for slavery as for safety, and count it not shame but highest honor to risk their blood and their lives for the vainglory of a tyrant; yet in a free state no more mischievous expedient could be planned or attempted. Wholly repugnant to the general freedom are such devices as enthralling men's minds with prejudice, forcing their judgment, or employing any of the weapons of quasi-religious sedition; indeed, such seditions only spring up, when law enters the domain of speculative thought, and opinions are put on trial and condemned on the same footing as crimes, while those who defend and follow them are sacrificed, not to public safety, but to their opponents' hatred and cruelty."

These lines from Spinoza's *Tractatus Theologico-Politicus* strikingly characterize the tragedy of our generation, with its noble patriotism degenerated into blind veneration of the nation-state idol.

Nothing can destroy the nationalist fetishes, prejudices and superstitions except the explosive power of common sense and rational thinking. Only a struggle in our minds can prevent further struggles on the battlefields.

The main reason advanced by our present government officials, legislators and political philosophers for continuing the nation-state structure, with all its disastrous consequences, is that people are "different." We are told that people cannot form a political entity until they are first "united in spirit," that it is impossible to shift loyalties and allegiances from national to supra-national objectives, that Latins and Anglo-Saxons, Slavs and Germans, and the many other racial, linguistic and national groups cannot be merged into a unified organization or placed under a common law.

These arguments, reiterated only too often by the most prominent representatives of the nation-states, are the shallowest of all contemporary sophisms.

Of course people are different.

If they were or could be "united in spirit," we would need no legal order, no state organization at all. It is precisely the differences between men, the profound differences of character, mentality, creed, language, traditions and ideals, which originally necessitated the introduction of law and a legal order in human society.

The assertion that the manifold differences existing in the human race prevent the creation of universal law and order is in flagrant contradiction to facts and to past and present realities.

Poles and Russians, Hungarians and Rumanians, Serbs and Bulgars, have disliked and distrusted each other and have been waging wars in Europe against each other for centuries. But these very same Poles and Russians, Hungarians and Rumanians, Serbs and Bulgars, once having left their countries and settled in the United States of America, cease fighting and are perfectly capable of living and working side by without waging wars against each other.

Why is this?

The biological, racial, religious, historic, temperamental and characteristic differences between them remain exactly the same.

The change in one factor alone produced the

miracle.

In Europe, sovereign power is vested in these nationalities and in their nation-states. In the United States of America, sovereign power resides, not in any one of these nationalities, but stands above them in the Union, under which individuals, irrespective of existing differences between them, are equal before the law.

The Germans and the French have distrusted and disliked each other and waged wars against each other for centuries. If any two peoples are different, they are indeed two different peoples. Their languages, mentalities, ideals, methods of thinking, ways of life, present great contrasts. If any two nations would seem incapable of unity, they are Germany and France.

And yet, situated between the powerful French and German nation-states—whose citizens have been warring with each other throughout their history—live about one million Frenchmen, as Gallic as any in the French Republic, and nearly three million Germans, as Germanic as any in the Reich, who have been living side by side in peace for long centuries while their kinsmen in the neighboring French and German states have periodically conquered and destroyed each other. The biological, racial, religious, cultural and mental differences between the inhabitants of Geneva and Lausanne, on the one side, and Bern, Zurich and Saint-Gall on the other, are exactly the same as are the biological, racial, religious cultural and mental differences between the inhabitants of

Paris, Bordeaux and Marseille on the one side, and Berlin, Munich and Dresden on the other.

Only one difference exists.

The French people in France and the German people in Germany live in sovereign nation-states where sovereignty is vested respectively in the French nation and in the German nation. In Switzerland, sovereignty is vested, not in the French nationality nor in the German nationality, but in the union of both, under which citizens belonging to either nationality enjoy equal protection, equal rights and equal obligations.

It seems, therefore, crystal-clear that friction, conflicts and wars between people are caused, not by their national, racial, religious, social and cultural differences, but by the *single fact* that these differences are galvanized in separate sovereignties which have no way to settle the conflicts resulting from their differences except through violent clashes.

Conflicts created by these same differences within the human race can be solved without violent clashes and wars whenever and wherever sovereignty resides, not in but above the conflicting units.

That mankind will ever be "united in spirit" or in interests is an utterly meaningless contention. It is not even desirable that such uniformity of mankind should ever be achieved. Uniformity would mean the end of culture and civilization.

The belief that the world can be united by a single movement—a religion, a language, a political creed, an economic system—has been predominant in the minds of fanatics all through history. It has been tried and tried again and has invariably failed. No conception is more erroneous than to believe that man must first be united in religion, culture, political outlook, economic methods, before he can be politically united in a state, a federation or any unified legal order.

Any attempt to impose one single cultural, religious, economic or philosophical conception upon all mankind is preposterous and implies an aggressive and totalitarian world outlook. The wide diversity among men and groups of men in the fields of philosophy, art, religion, language, political and economic methods, constitutes the very essence of culture. These differences not only should be cherished but must be protected in every possible way. All through history, however, such differences have always been self-destructive when the different groups enjoyed absolute sovereignty and were not protected by a higher source of law.

A universal legal order, so badly needed by the world today, far from endangering in any way these cultural differences, is the condition for the maintenance and continuous thriving of such differences. Without union, either the Scots would have exterminated the English or the English would have exterminated the Scots, just as the Romans destroyed Carthage and the Huns destroyed Rome. Within the United Kingdom, the Scots are more Scottish in their traditions and character, and the English are more English in theirs, than they ever were before that union when they were killing each other.

Another fallacy is that two different economic systems, two different conceptions of economic order, such as Communism in Soviet Russia and capitalism in the West, cannot be integrated within one system of law, within one society.

In France, England, Switzerland and Holland, the telephone, telegraph, electric light services and many other economic operations are conducted on a communist basis, owned by the state or other communal collectivities, just as in the Soviet Union, and are not private enterprises as in the U.S.A. On the other hand, textile, chemical, machine tool and other factories in these very same countries are privately owned as in the U.S.A. and not by the government as in the U.S.S.R.

How can collectively and privately owned enterprises coexist in one state, under one system of law? Very well indeed, as the example of England, France, Switzerland and Holland prove.

Even in the United States, the most completely capitalist-individualist country, we see government created and government-owned enterprises operating smoothly and advantageously side by side with private enterprises, as the Tennessee Valley Administration and many other public works demonstrate. And should the people of the United States some day decide that the Federal government take over telephone service from the Bell Telephone Company, telegraph service from

Western Union, railroads from the many individual private companies, this would in no way endanger or interfere with private ownership and privately managed industries in other fields.

Different economic conceptions, different economic systems, can perfectly well coexist within one political and social system, under one sovereignty. In fact, the *only* way they can coexist peacefully is within one legal system.

The widespread belief that any unified legal order between the Soviet Union and the Western democracies is impossible because of the fundamental differences in their economic systems, is no more valid than the century-old prejudice that Catholics and Protestants could not live peacefully in the same community.

What makes the Communist economy of Soviet Russia "dangerous" to the West, and what makes the capitalist system of the Western countries "dangerous" to the U.S.S.R. is not the difference in their economic systems but the fact that these different economic systems are incorporated in different sovereign states and are separate sovereignties. It is the Soviet nation-state that is a threat to the West and it is the Western nation-states that are a menace to the Soviet Union. Not because of hostile intentions, but because of their very existence as sovereign units.

Conflicts between these sovereign nation-states are inevitable, not because of differences in their economic methods and in their economic systems, but because of the nonintegrated sovereign power of the divided social units.

In every document, agreement, charter or communiqué they issue, our statesmen stubbornly persist in declaring that they want peace by safeguarding and guaranteeing "the sovereign equality of all nations." They are unable to realize the contradiction inherent in this eternally repeated, meaningless slogan. The coexistence of social groups with equal sovereign power is precisely the condition of war, the very condition that can never, under any circumstances, bring peace.

Far from being an obstacle to a unified legal order, the differences between the Russian and Western economic systems make an over-all, unified, sovereign legal order *imperative* if we want to prevent a violent clash between them.

One thing is certain. No number of joint declarations of good will, military alliances, mutual nonaggression pacts, divisions of spheres of influence, conferences between the leaders, banquets, toasts and fireworks, will ever prevent the impending and inevitable clash between sovereign social units.

The major and most widespread argument against the establishment of inter-national law is that it "just cannot be." There is no gainsaying the logic and the practical demand for such a world order, but it "just cannot be..."

No debate is possible with this class of eternal skeptics. They bring to mind an old story. According to legend, Pythagoras, after his discovery that the sum of the angles of any triangle is equal to two right angles, out of gratitude to the gods sacrificed one hundred oxen. Since that time, all oxen become panic-stricken and low in fear when anything new is in sight.

All those nationalist forces which, in 1919, fought against Wilson's League, after having witnessed its inefficacy during two decades, now fervently advocate its restoration in the form of another organization composed of sovereign nations.

The argument of those who want a repetition of this historic failure is indeed strange. They say:

1. Our purpose is to prevent a third world war.
2. Any measure proposed which would involve delegation of parts of the sovereignty of the peoples to democratically controlled bodies higher than the nation-states is *impractical* because:
3. Such proposals would not be accepted by the present governments of the nation-states.

The persistent opposition to reason and logic in political matters from those who have no other argument but "practicality" is the most vulgar manifestation of human mind and behavior. It would never be tolerated if the conduct of human affairs were based on principles and guided by reason.

If our purpose is to prevent another world war, then the practicality or impracticality of a proposed method can be judged only in relation to the object sought: Can it or can it not prevent another world war?

It is nonsense and illogical to say that a method

proposed to prevent another world war is impractical because of a third element in this peculiar logical construction, namely: because it will not be accepted by the national governments now holding power.

If our purpose is to devise methods acceptable to the existing governments of the nation-states, there can be no disputing that only methods acceptable to these national governments are to be regarded as practical.

But then let us be frank and say that such is our purpose.

Let us not continue to mislead the public by saying that such methods will prevent a third world war. They will not.

What is the meaning of the word "practical" in political affairs?

Is it something that is actually happening, which is actually being done in our lifetime? In this case, nothing is more practical than war. Misery is practical, suffering is practical, killing, deportation, oppression, persecution, starvation are essentially practical. It would seem that our endeavor should be to eliminate these practices from society. They are inseparably linked with the nation-state structure of society, of which they are the direct outcome.

How is it possible to measure the practicality or impracticality of an ideal, of a doctrine, of a program aimed at eradicating these evils, by whether or not they are acceptable to the very same institutions from which emanate the evils we seek to destroy?

Those who cannot understand the fundamental difference between a universal legal order and a league or a council usually urge us to be "practical." If the people and the governments are not ready or willing to accept more than a council composed of sovereign nation-states, then let us at least take that, runs the argument. Let us make a first step, a beginning.

It is most reasonable to start by taking a "first step." The trouble with league-council proposals, however, is that a league or a council does not initiate anything.

It is not a first step. It is a continuation. A continuation of error, of a fatally bad and disastrous policy.

It is a negative step. It is a step away from our goal. If we want peace between the nations, then a council of sovereign nations takes us backwards. A council of sovereign nations artificially prolongs the life of the nation-state structure and in consequence is a step toward war.

The "practical men" who preach that a world organization of sovereign nation-states is a realistic approach to our problem are the finest specimens of those eternal political reactionaries Disraeli once defined: "A practical man is a man who practices the error of his forefathers."

The innumerable international conferences, which are held almost every month, are nothing but the epileptic convulsions of the incurably infirm system of nation-states. Every few weeks a

new crisis arises in which "public opinion" childishly clamors for another meeting of the leaders,
expecting a miracle—an agreement between the
national governments that would cure the disease.
Every time, they get an empty, insignificant "communiqué" that poultices the immediate pain for a
while, but within a month or less, another issue
becomes acute, for which no remedy is known except another conference.

All these meetings of representatives of sovereign national governments are bound to be futile,
as they take place on a level altogether different
from where the real problem lies. Within such a
council of sovereign nation-states, no other course
is possible than that which has been followed in
the past.

And we know that nonintervention in international conflicts always and necessarily means
positive intervention on the side of the stronger
belligerent to the detriment of the weaker.

We know that the policy of "balance of power"
can maintain peace between nations only so long
as power is *not in balance.* Only as long as one
nation or one group of nations has supremacy
over the other. In such a system, as soon as power
between the two opposing groups is really "in
balance," war is imminent and inevitable.

And we also know that the policy of spheres of
influence is bound to develop into a policy which
seeks influence in the spheres of others.

It is in the light of these facts that one can judge
the value of the new term which is supposed to

have a devastating effect upon those who have had
enough of living under constant threat of being
murdered, robbed, persecuted and oppressed by
the nation-states and who would like to live a
civilized life in peace under law. The term is:
"Perfectionism."

Anyone who does not believe in the "first step
theory" of the United Nations Organization is
branded a "perfectionist." And "perfectionism," of
course, is the most dangerous of all political vices.

No one knows when a universal legal order will
be achieved and no doubt all who are striving
toward that ideal would be perfectly satisfied with
a modest "first step"—toward it. But the fact is
that our governments have not even indicated an
intention ever to take a first step in that direction.

A man wanting to go from New York to Rio de
Janeiro, who discovers after leaving the harbor
that he has been taken on a boat headed for
Southampton, cannot find much consolation in
learning that the boat will make a "first stop" at
Cherbourg. He is being taken in an opposite direction to that which he wishes. Is it dangerous
perfectionism if he insists that it is not to Cherbourg but to Rio de Janeiro that he wants to go?

War is the result of unregulated contact between
power units.

Regionalism will only accelerate the tempo of
war. If we organize sovereign nation-states in
regional groups, then all nations of a region will
be in contact with all nations in the other regions,
and if relations between the regions remain on a

basis of regional or national sovereignty then we shall have war.

Did the German Reich, the regional federation of the German states, bring peace? Has the regional federation of England, Scotland and Wales, or that of the forty-eight American states protected their peoples from war?

Most assuredly, these regional federations stopped once and for all the wars that had raged *between* the once sovereign units that had merged to become a federation. Since their union, the peoples of the newly formed regional sovereign federations no longer needed to go into battle against each other. But together, *as a regional unit,* they continued to be exposed to war, for the identical reason that had caused wars among themselves, before their federation. Irrespective of the federations of regional groups, there continued to exist several sovereign power units with which the regional federations were not integrated and with which they remained in contact.

Today, the interdependence of all the nations on this small planet is so complete that federations of regions—although they would end wars *within* the federated regions—cannot possibly protect the peoples from violent conflicts *between* the different federations, if each regional unit remains sovereign unto itself and if the relations of these sovereign regional units continue to be regulated, not by law but by the old, fallacious methods of diplomacy, foreign policy and representation in an inter-national or inter-regional council.

The problem is not how to bring together nations which are neighbors, which are of similar heritage and which like each other. The problem is how to make possible the peaceful coexistence of peoples who are different and who dislike each other.

Those who can find no argument against the logical and urgent necessity of transforming the institutions of national sovereignty into institutions capable of creating and maintaining law, not only within nations but also between them, and yet are reluctant or unwilling to accept responsibility, seek escape in the argument that the time is not yet ripe for such reforms. Perhaps in five hundred years...Perhaps in one hundred years...Perhaps during the next generation—they waver. But not *we* and not *now*.

The truth is that ever since the beginning of the twentieth century these reforms have been overdue.

If we used our brains for the purpose for which they were created—for thinking—and if we let our actions be guided by principles arrived at by rational thinking, these changes in our society would have been carried out before the events of 1914. The outbreak of the first World War was the clearly visible symptom that this opportunity had been missed and that the crisis resulting from the clash between realities and institutions was entering an acute stage.

The series of violent upheavals and concussions which, following the first World War, for the first time in history simultaneously engulfed the entire globe in an ever-increasing crescendo, culminating in the unparalleled explosions of the second World War, are symptoms which show, more clearly than any man could describe, the inadequacy, inefficiency and senility of the institutions by which we allow ourselves to be governed.

The same Winston Churchill who, when the darkest hour was over and the Battle of Britain won, subscribed to the Atlantic Charter and all the other documents and declarations that are leading us astray and strengthening the nation-state structure for the next war, once performed an act of statesmanship which makes any excuse for taking the wrong course now seem perfectly ridiculous. In the hour of gravest peril, when Hitler's hordes were victoriously trampling the soil of France, on the very eve of French capitulation, on June 16, 1940, the British Ambassador to France handed the following draft declaration to the French government:

At this most fateful moment in the history of the modern world, the Governments of the United Kingdom and the French Republic make this declaration of indissoluble union and unyielding resolution in their common defence of justice and freedom against subjection to a system which reduces mankind to a life of robots and slaves.

The two Governments declare that France and Great Britain shall no longer be two nations but one Franco-British Union. The constitution of the Union will provide for joint organs of defence, foreign, financial and economic policies. Every citizen of

France will enjoy immediate citizenship of Great Britain, every British subject will become a citizen of France.

Both countries will share responsibility for the repair of the devastation of war, wherever it occurs in their territories, and the resources of both shall be equally, and as one, applied to that purpose.

During the war there shall be a single war Cabinet, and all the forces of Britain and France, whether on land, sea or in the air, will be placed under its direction. It will govern from wherever it best can. The two Parliaments will be formally associated.

The nations of the British Empire are already forming new armies. France will keep her available forces in the field, on the sea, and in the air.

The Union appeals to the United States to fortify the economic resources of the Allies and to bring her powerful material aid to the common cause.

The Union will concentrate its whole energy against the power of the enemy no matter where the battle may be. And thus we shall conquer.

This proposal of union between France and Great Britain embodies the fundamental principles of future society, as opposed to the principles of the past expressed in the Covenant of the League of Nations, the Atlantic Charter, the Dumbarton Oaks and San Francisco documents. And it was a *concrete, official* proposal made by the British government, presided over by Winston Churchill, to the government of the French Republic. Of course, it came at a hopelessly inopportune moment. France had already received a death blow from the German Army. The Third Republic was disintegrating. A few hours later it died.

In view of this historic event, how can it be said that "the time is not yet ripe" for measures which were actually and officially proposed by the British government to the French government, as the only salvation in a desperate extremity? Is it too much to expect that people who, at the point of death and when it is too late, are willing to take the remedy, will make use of that very same remedy when still in possession of their full senses and when there is still time for it to be effective? Or must we become resigned and admit that Plato was right in saying that "human beings never make laws; it is the accidents and catastrophes of all kinds, happening in every conceivable way, that make the laws for us"?

The institution of the sovereign nation-state has been dead now for several decades. We cannot revive it by refusing to bury the corpse.

There are a number of people holding high government office or chairs in universities who understand perfectly the underlying problem of peace but who indulge in the puerile excuse that "the time is not yet ripe."

History never asks rulers and representatives of an existing regime when they will consent to institute the reforms made necessary by progress. Those who have succeeded, rarely see the need for change nor of what it will consist. Often in the past, reforms that seemed imminent were delayed for centuries; on the other hand, reforms regarded as utopian became realities overnight. The great majority of the living never realize the fundamental changes taking place during their lifetime.

How can we expect from our governments and from the self-appointed interpreters of public opinion in universities, in radio or in the press, any greater insight into what is going on today than was shown by their predecessors in other similarly revolutionary eras? Those who can visualize the realities of tomorrow only in things and beliefs already existing today will never be able to solve our problem, will never be capable of searching for principles nor of shaping the future according to the principles of tomorrow.

Anatole France tells this wise and profound story in *Sur la Pierre Blanche:*

In the days of Nero, in the prosperous Greek city of Corinth, the Roman proconsul Gallion, was discussing the future of the world with some of his Roman and Greek friends, statesmen and scientists. They all agreed that nobody believed any longer in the old gods, neither in Egyptian, nor Babylonian, nor Greek, nor Roman gods. The question was raised: What will be the new religion? Who will succeed Jupiter? The distinguished and cultured gathering spiritedly debated the chances of about a dozen new gods, when the delightful conversation was interrupted by a noisy quarrel between a strange, haggard Jew—one Saul or Paul of Tarsus—and a rabbi of the synagogue who accused Paul of revolutionizing the existing law. After the unpleasant incident, Gallion and his

friends spent a few moments discussing the queer
and ridiculous faith that this Paul was spreading,
the teaching of an obscure Jewish prophet called
Chrestus, or Cherestus, who had caused so much
trouble to another Roman proconsul in Judea.
One of the guests jokingly wondered if this Chrestus might not succeed Jupiter. The idea greatly
amused everyone. They unanimously agreed that
this would be absurd indeed. The chances were all
in favor of Hercules...

CHAPTER XV

LAW ... CONQUEST

Our Laws and Statutes are inherited
From generation to generation,
And spread slowly from place to place
Like a disease that has no end.
Reason to folly, blessings to curses
Turn. Woe be to us! Heirs of all the Past,
For to our Birthrights, born with us,
No one gives heed!...No one, alas!

(GOETHE: *Faust*)

THE problem of our twentieth century crisis,
seemingly so vastly complex and inextricable
with its hundreds of national, territorial, religious,
social, economic, political and cultural riddles, can
be reduced to a few simple propositions.

1. From the teachings of history we have learned that conflicts and wars between social units are inevitable whenever and wherever groups of men with equal sovereignty come into contact.

2. Whenever and wherever social units in any field, regardless of size and character, have come into contact and the resulting friction has led to war, we have learned that these conflicts have always ceased after some part of the sovereignty of the warring units was transferred to a higher social unit able to create legal order, a government authority under which the previously warring groups became equal members of a broader society and within which conflicts between groups could be controlled and eradicated by legal means without the use of force.

3. From the experience thus gained we know that within any given group of individuals in contact and communication with each other, conflict is inevitable whenever and wherever sovereign power resides in the individual members or groups of members of society, and not in society itself.

4. We further know that, irrespective of the immediate and apparent causes of conflict among warring groups, these causes ceased producing wars and violent conflicts only through the establishment of a legal order, only when the social groups in conflict were subjected to a superior system of law, and that, in all cases and at all times, the effect of such a superior system of law

has been the cessation of the use of violence among the previously warring groups.

5. Knowing that wars between nonintegrated social groups in contact are inevitable, that the coexistence of nonintegrated sovereign social groups always and in all cases has led to wars, we must realize that peace among men, among individuals, or among groups of individuals in any sphere, is the result of legal order. Peace is identical with the existence of law.

6. As the twentieth century crisis is a world-wide clash between the social units of sovereign nation-states, the problem of peace in our time is the establishment of a legal order to regulate relations among men, beyond and above the nation-states. This requires transferring parts of the sovereign authority of the existing warring national institutions to universal institutions capable of creating law and order in human relations beyond and above the nation-states.

These propositions are merely the reduction into elementary formulas of one long line of events in our history. The task before us is nothing unique. It is one step further in the same direction, the next step in our evolution.

That conditions in our present society make it imperative for us to undertake this step without further delay should by now be clear to everybody.

Within a single generation, two world wars have ravaged mankind, interfered with peaceful progress and disrupted the free, democratic way of life of the entire Western world. In spite of the desire of the overwhelming majority of the peoples to live and work in peace, we have been unable to escape war. For more than three decades, we have been witnessing an unprecedented decay and downfall of our civilization.

To wage this stupendous struggle, we have had to submit to a hitherto unknown degree of privation, persecution, degradation, suffering, and have been forced to change drastically our civilized way of life. The great majority of the entire human race has been subjected to regimentation, dictation, fear, serfdom.

Considering this world-shaking catastrophe which directly affects every home and every individual,

We believe that the progress of science and industry have rendered national authorities powerless to safeguard the people against armed aggression or to prevent devastating wars.

We believe that peace in any country of the world cannot be maintained without the existence of an effective universal government organization to prevent crime in the inter-national field.

We believe that independence of a nation does not mean untrammeled and unrestricted freedom to do whatever it wants, and that real independence can be created only if no nation is free to attack another, to drag it into war, and to cause such devastating loss of life and wealth as has been wrought twice in our lifetime.

We believe that security of a nation, just as

security of an individual, means the co-operation of all to secure the rights of each.

We believe that the relations between nations, just as the relations between individuals in a community, can be peaceful only if based upon and regulated by Law.

We believe that the only way to prevent future world wars is through regulation of the inter-relationship of nations, not by unenforceable treaty obligations, which sovereign nations will always disregard, but by an enforceable legal order, binding all nations, giving all nationals equal rights under the established law, and imposing equal obligations upon each.

We believe that peace and security can be established and assured only if we, the sovereign people, who, for our own safety and well-being have delegated parts of our sovereignty to cities to handle our municipal affairs, to departments, counties, provinces, cantons or states to take care of departmental, county, provincial, cantonal or state issues, to our national governments to attend to our national problems—to protect ourselves against the danger of inter-national wars, now delegate part of our respective sovereignty to bodies capable of creating and applying Law in inter-national relations.

We believe that we can protect ourselves against inter-national wars only through the establishment of constitutional life in world affairs, and that such universal Law must be created in conformity with the democratic process, by freely elected and responsible representatives. Creation, application and execution of the Law must be rigorously controlled by the democratic process.

We believe that only a world-wide legal order can insure freedom from fear, and make possible the unhindered development of economic energies for the achievement of freedom from want.

We believe that the natural and inalienable rights of man must prevail. Under twentieth century realities they can be preserved only if they are protected by Law against destruction from outside forces.

How can these propositions be translated into institutions and become the driving force of political reality?

Nothing is more futile than to work out detailed plans and prepare drafts for a constitutional document of a world government. It would be a simple matter for a competent individual or group of people to sit down and work out scores of plans in all detail and in all variety. Within a few days one could produce twenty constitutional drafts, each completely different from the others, each equally plausible.

Such procedure would only hinder progress. Nothing is more open to criticism than a constitution, unless it be the draft of a constitution.

If at the very inception of democracy, before the democratic nation-states had been created in the eighteenth century, a specific draft of a democratic constitution had been identified with democracy itself, and put forward for general approval and acceptance, we should never have had a democratic nation-state anywhere in the world.

History does not work that way.

The founders of democracy were much wiser and more politic. They first formulated a small number of fundamental principles regarded as self-evident and basic for a democratic society. These principles succeeded in arousing the vision and inflaming the enthusiasm of the peoples who, on the basis of these fundamental principles, empowered their representatives to translate them into reality and create the machinery necessary for a permanent legal order, representing the triumph of these principles.

The constitutions, the fundamental laws of the new democratic order, were debated *after,* not before the acceptance of the elementary principles and the mandate given by the people to their representatives for the realization of those principles. So today we see democracy expressed in systems of great variety in detail, but nonetheless, deriving from identical principles.

Democracy in the United States is different from British democracy. French democracy is different from the Dutch, and Swiss democracy has institutions differing greatly from Swedish democracy. In spite of their differences in detail, they are all workable forms of democracy, expressing the same fundamental social conception, the sovereignty of the people as understood a hundred and fifty years ago.

Regarding the creation of universal democratic legal order, we have not yet reached the stage of conception. We have not yet formulated the principles. We have not yet set the standards.

To put the problem before national governments would be a hopeless enterprise, doomed to failure before even starting. The representatives of the sovereign nation-states are incapable of acting and thinking otherwise than according to their nation-centric conceptions. As such a universal problem cannot be solved along national lines, certainly and naturally they would destroy any plan, any draft, of a universal legal order.

Our national statesmen and legislators, by virtue of their education, mentality and outlook, are completely insensitive to the nature of the reform required. Besides, many high priests of the nation-state cult look upon international war as an admirable instrument of advancement toward wealth, fame, distinction and immortality.

Waging war is the easiest thing in the world. It is a business which has a clearly defined, primitive aim—to destroy the adversary—and is based on simple arithmetic and strategy, easy to learn. To manage an enterprise in which one can spend unlimited amounts of money regardless of income, produce goods irrespective of markets, monopolize newspaper space and radio time for self-advertisement, enjoy dictatorial powers over lives and property, establish an artificial, *ad hoc* hierarchy and a high command that suppresses all criticism, seize all means of production and communication, creates a situation which ought to satisfy the caesarmania of any child. Many of our ministers, generals, diplomats, scientists, engineers, poets and manufacturers—consciously or unconsciously— just adore wars. At no other time is it so easy to achieve success, so easy to obtain the applause and servile adulation of the rabble.

All these people, while constantly paying pious tribute to "peace," are solidly entrenched in the hierarchy of the nation-state, and will defend to the last the fetishes, taboos and superstitions of a society with such unparalleled opportunities for them.

From men who are personal beneficiaries of the old system—incapable of independent thinking and victims of the scandalous method of teaching history in all the civilized countries—we cannot expect constructive ideas, much less constructive measures.

We must therefore begin at the beginning. And the beginning is the Word.

This should in no way be discouraging. In this modern world of ours, with mass-circulation news-papers, motion pictures and radio, capable of reaching the entire civilized population of the earth, a decade is ample time for a movement to bring to triumph the principles of universal law, if such a movement is guided by men who have learned from the churches and the political parties how to propagate ideas and how to build up a dynamic organization behind an idea.

The crisis of the twentieth century conclusively demonstrates that democracy and industrialism can no longer coexist in a nation-state.

If we insist upon maintaining the nation-state framework and want to continue with industrial progress, we are bound to arrive at totalitarian Fascism.

If we believe that a free, democratic way of life is what we want, and that an intensification of industrialism and mass production is what we need, then we must remove the barrier blocking the road to that goal, and replace the archaic nation-state structure with a universal legal order in which development toward political and economic freedom and wealth can become a reality.

If we are determined to maintain the nation-state framework and at the same time endeavor to preserve democracy, we shall be forced to give up industrial progress, reduce populations and return to a rural way of life.

As this Rousseau-like dream of a return to nature is unthinkable, it can be excluded. The alternative for the future of modern society is: totalitarianism within the nation-state framework under treaty arrangements, or democracy under universal law, under government. But for that government to be democratic, there must first be a government.

The longing for security within the nation-state structure is the most dangerous of all collective drives. In the small, interdependent world of today, there are only two ways for a nation to achieve security.

Law ... Conquest.

As the nation-state structure excludes a legal order embracing men living in different sovereign units, the drive for security directly produces the drive for conquest.

The drive for security is the major cause of imperialism.

This has never been admitted by the representatives of those powers who have actually traveled that road.

It is amusing to hear the anti-imperialist diatribes of the representatives of the two most virulently imperialist nations of the middle twentieth century—U.S.A. and U.S.S.R. Both nations are persuaded that they are anti-imperialist and that what they want is nothing but security. To understand this paradox, it is most enlightening to reread the history of the growth of the Roman Empire.

Nobody in Rome wanted an empire, nobody wanted war, nobody was an imperialist. They merely liked and valued their own civilization, their higher culture and standard of living, and were anxious to preserve their own way of life. The dominating conception was as "isolationist" as that of any midwestern Senator in Washington or central Russian Commissar in Moscow. The Romans wanted only to be left alone, to enjoy their higher living standards, their superior civilization.

But unfortunately, the barbarians on their frontiers did not leave them alone and always made trouble for them in one way or another. So their deep desire for security forced the Romans to go beyond their frontiers, to eliminate immediate dangers and to push their frontiers farther away from Rome to protect themselves. This desire for security led them finally to conquer virtually all of the then known world and to subjugate other peoples, until internal decay and new, stronger outside forces finally destroyed the whole structure.

This is the real story of most of the great empires of world history. It is also the story of the British Empire, which has been built up by the desire for security of British commercial investments and interests scattered all over the world, of growing British industrialism, which was essential to the survival of the British Isles.

Today this very same force is the driving element behind the policy of the Soviet Union and the United States. Both are deeply convinced of the superiority of their own values and standards and the primacy of their own civilizations. They have vast territories and are not in need of expansion *per se.* Their sincere desire is to be left alone, to live peacefully and to be able to continue to live their own way of life.

But the globe is shrinking, steppes and oceans are no longer safe frontiers, and other nations are not willing to let them do what they want. Outside forces constantly threaten and occasionally attack them. Therefore, to achieve security they feel obliged to build up huge armed forces, to defeat and conquer their immediate enemies and to push ahead their ramparts, their defense positions, their bases, their spheres of influence, farther and farther.

At the end of the second World War, we are seeing American forces annexing islands and other bases thousands of miles away from the American mainland for reasons of security. And we are seeing the Soviet frontiers pushed forward from the Arctic to the Mediterranean and from Europe to the Far East, also for defensive reasons.

It is no use accusing the Soviet or the American governments of imperialism. They sincerely believe that these measures are purely security measures. Just as sincerely they are convinced that superior armed force in the hands of any other nation would be dangerous to peace, but a guarantee of peace and a benefit for all in their own possession. And they are equally sincere in believing that the dissemination of their own political doctrines in other nations, the acceptance by other nations of their own political and economic conceptions, would strengthen peace and would be beneficial to all.

All these unmistakable symptoms of present-day realities indicate that if we insist upon remaining on the old road of national sovereignty, the drive for security, inherent in all nations, will push us toward more violent clashes between the nation-states, compared to which the first and second world wars will appear as child's play.

After the liquidation of the second World War, there remain only three powers capable of creating and maintaining armed forces in the modern sense: three empires. The small and medium-sized nations will inescapably have to become satellites of one of these three dominating industrial and military powers.

Some incurable dreamers among our statesmen seriously believe that such a triangular power structure of our world is possible—even desirable. Actually, it is the mathematical formula for the next, probably the last phase of the struggle for the conquest of the world.

In spite of the endlessly repeated anti-imperialist catch phrases of the representatives of the great powers, every economic and technological reality of our epoch, every dynamic force in the world today, every law of history and logic, indicates that we are on the verge of a period of empire building—of aggregations more powerful and more centralized than ever before. There is no virtue in relying on obsolete slogans and ignoring the forces that today are pushing mankind toward a more organized control of this earth.

It would be wiser to recognize these realities and to guide the torrent into democratic channels. If we leave the concept of sovereign nationalities enshrined as the test of "freedom" the contradiction between this fiction and the physical facts will only cause greater explosions. Unless interdependence, and hence the need for the centralized rule of law—for the freedom which comes from equality before the law among nations as among individuals—is recognized, we shall suffer further and more devastating wars among the United States, Great Britain, Soviet Russia and whatever other nation-states retain any sizable power, in every possible combination. As in an elimination contest, one of these or a combination will achieve by force that unified control made mandatory by the times we live in. Of course, it will be a strictly anti-imperialist imperialism, a kind of very anti-Fascist Fascism. Intervention will always take place in the name of nonintervention, oppression will be called protection and vassalage will be established by solemnly assuring the conquered nation its right to choose the form of government it wants.

There is something angelic in the simplicity and credulity of professional statesmen.

What the two camps destined to wage the coming struggle for conquest of the world are going to say about each other's political intentions, social and economic systems, how they will explain to others and justify to themselves the causes of the war—fought, naturally, in sheer self-defense and for self-preservation by both sides—will be sentimental claptrap. Pure doggerel...It will have not the slightest relation to facts.

In spite of frequent repetitions and parallels, there exist a great number of unique phenomena in human history.

From the beginning of history until our days, until the exploration of the Arctic and Antarctic, people have discovered new continents, new lands, new islands. But this seemingly permanent characteristic of past history is now at an end. The era of geographic discovery is closed. It is almost certain that we know every corner of this globe and that no new lands await the arrival of adventurous navigators. For the first time since man's history has been recorded, we possess our entire globe. Until and unless we are able to communicate with another planet, the theater of human history will be limited to geographically determined, constant and known dimensions.

With this unique and radical change in our geographical and political outlook, expansion, growth, conquest and colonization are no longer possible in virgin territories, but only at each other's expense. During the past five centuries, competition in conquest was possible without necessarily encroaching upon the possessions of other powers, through discovery and annexation of new lands, with occasional naval encounters or local armed skirmishes to discourage a competitor.

This period of history is now over. National security, the urge for conquest, can be satisfied only by subjugating and appropriating territories and possessions of other nations, thereby destroying their security.

Until today throughout its entire history, the world was too vast to be conquered by a single man or a single power. Technical means have always lagged behind the objective. The world was always too large to be conquered entirely, even by the greatest force.

The planet was too elastic, it seemed to grow constantly. Alexander, Caesar, Genghis Khan, the Spaniards, the English, Napoleon—all failed. They all conquered a large part of the world, but never the entire world.

Now only, for the first time in history, the conquest of the world by a single power is a geographic, technical and military possibility.

The world cannot grow any more, it is a known quantity.

As discoveries ended, the growth of the world was suddenly brought to a standstill. Technical developments rapidly caught up and made the globe smaller and smaller. Today the world is completely engulfed by modern industrialism. From a technical and military point of view, the world of today is considerably smaller than was the territory held by any one of the major empires of the past centuries. It is infinitely easier and quicker for the United States to wage war in the Far East than it was for Caesar to do so in Anglia or Egypt.

Modern science has made war a highly mechanized art which can be mastered only by the major industrial powers.

Only three of these are left.

And any one of the three, by defeating the other two, would conquer and rule the world.

For the first time in human history, *one* power

can conquer and rule the world. Indeed but for the industrial potential of the United States, Hitler might have done it! Developments may take a different turn. But technically and militarily, it is a definite possibility.

And politically, it is a definite probability if no legal order is created to satisfy the instinctive desire of peoples for security. A decision upon this crucial issue will probably be reached before the end of the twentieth century.

To put it bluntly, the meaning of the crisis of the twentieth century is that this planet must to some degree be brought under unified control. Our task, our duty, is to attempt to institute this unified control in a democratic way by first proclaiming its principles, and to achieve it by persuasion and with the least possible bloodshed. If we fail to accomplish this, we can be certain that the iron law of history will compel us to wage more and more wars, with more and more powerful weapons, against more and more powerful groups, until unified control is finally attained through conquest.

Political unification of the world by conquest is expensive, painful, bloody. The goal could be achieved so much more easily if it were not for that eternal saboteur of progress—human blindness.

But if it is impossible to cure that blindness and if mankind is unable to face its destiny and to determine by reason and insight the course of our immediate future, if our nationalist dogmatism will not permit us to undertake the organization of a universal legal order, then at least, let us try not to prolong the agony of a decaying, dying system of society.

If we cannot attain to universalism and create union by common consent and democratic methods as a result of rational thinking—then rather than retard the process, let us precipitate unification by conquest. It serves no reasonable purpose to prolong the death throes of our decrepit institutions and to postpone inevitable events only to make the changes more painful and more costly in blood and suffering. It would be better to have done with this operation as quickly as possible so that the fight for the reconquest of lost human liberties can start within the universal state without too much loss of time.

The era of inter-national wars will end, just as everything human ends. It will come to an end with the establishment of universal law to regulate human relationship, either by union or by—conquest.

The modern Bastille is the nation-state, no matter whether the jailers are conservative, liberal or socialist. That symbol of our establishment must be destroyed if we ever want to be free again. The great revolution for the liberation of man has to be fought all over again.

Nothing characterizes the intellectual poverty and the creative sterility of our generation more than the fact that Communism is regarded as the most revolutionary force of the time. Exactly what is revolutionary in Communism?

Revolution does not mean merely to fight an existing order, a system, parties and men actually in power. It does not mean merely to shoot or to use violence to overthrow a regime. The "have nots" will always fight the "haves"; those who are without influence will always oppose the powerful. But that is not revolution.

Revolution means the clear recognition of the roots of the evils of society at any given moment, the concentration of all forces to exterminate these roots, and to replace a sick society by a new social order that no longer produces the causes of the evils of the previous regime.

Communism—today an ultranationalist force—does not recognize and does not combat the ultimate source of the misery of our age: the institution of the sovereign nation-state. Bureaucracy, militarism, war, unemployment, poverty, persecution, oppression—all that Communism attributes to capitalism—are in reality products and effects of the nation-state structure of the world. In the middle of the twentieth century, no movement can be regarded as revolutionary that does not concentrate its action and its might on eradicating that tyrannical institution which, for its own self-perpetuation and self-glorification, transforms men into murderers and slaves.

An essential characteristic of every really revolutionary movement in history is that it breaks down barriers and creates more human freedom. Often this was done by violence, bloodshed, terror. But these are not characteristics of revolutions. Movements producing violence, bloodshed and terror are not revolutionary, if they do not aim at creating more freedom. If they actually create less freedom, they are counter-revolutionary, reactionary, even if they apply revolutionary slogans and tactics and produce violence, bloodshed and terror.

Communism, as its doctrine was formulated in the early part of the nineteenth century and as it is practiced by the Stalin regime in the Soviet Union, has absolutely nothing revolutionary in the real sense of the word. The doctrine ignored the real problem. And the practice, far from solving it, has created one of the most formidable Bastilles of the *ancien régime,* against which must be concentrated all the truly progressive and revolutionary forces of the middle twentieth century.

That our generation has not yet produced a creed and a movement more radical and revolutionary than the creed and movement which were considered radical and revolutionary in the time of Victoria, Napoleon III and Bismarck, is a fact this generation should feel deeply ashamed of.

We must search for the truth about peace and its possibilities, regardless of whether certain dogmas and fetishes now cherished permit or do not permit its immediate realization. We must understand quite clearly what peace is and how a peaceful order can be set up. Then it will be up to the people to decide whether they want it or not.

But we can no longer afford to believe in false conceptions, in utopias, in miracles. We can no longer afford to believe that a piece of paper, or even parchment, called a treaty and signed by the representatives of groups of people enjoying absolute sovereignty, can ever secure peace for any considerable period, no matter what the content of the treaty may be.

History, like botany and zoology, teaches us the inescapable and immutable law of nature, which applies to everything living, including human society. There is either growth or decay. There is no such thing as immutability, there is nothing static in this world of ours.

The only historical meaning, the only usefulness that can be conceded to a league of nations, or indeed to any organization of nation-states with equal sovereignty, is to illustrate that utopian structures based on "good will," "lasting friendship," "unity of purpose," "common interest" or on any similar fiction cannot work. The Confederation of the thirteen American states, with each state jealously guarding its full and untrammeled sovereignty, was historically justified only by the proof it gave that it could not work, that the peaceful coexistence of the peoples of the thirteen states and the guarantee of their individual security lay in the Union.

But after all the catastrophic events that

followed the foundation of the League of Nations, is it really necessary to create another league—a hotbed for coming global wars—to prove that it cannot work? Are not the first and second world wars enough "experience"? Do we really need a third global war to understand the anatomy of peace and to see what causes war in human society and how it can be prevented?

Let us be clear about one thing. A league of sovereign nation-states is not a step, neither the first step nor the ninety-ninth, toward peace. Peace is law. The San Francisco league is the pitiful miscarriage of the second World War. We shall have to organize peace independently of the Unholy Alliance stillborn in San Francisco or else we shall delude ourselves by believing in a miracle, until the inevitable march of events into another and greater holocaust teaches us that equal and sovereign power units can never, under any circumstances, under any conditions, coexist peacefully.

After dissecting the body of human society and seeing clearly the anatomy of peace, one is compelled to cry out in desperation: Must we blindly and helplessly endure the coming Armageddon between the surviving giant nation-states to endow the world with a constitution?

After a disastrous half a century of antirationalism, guided by mysticism, transcendental emotions and so-called intuition, we must return to the lost road of rationalism, if we want to prevent complete destruction of our civilization.

The task is by no means easy. The deceptions caused by rationalism are real and understandable. Yet, to try to escape the complexities of life revealed to us by reason by seeking refuge in irrationalism and to let our actions be determined by superstitions, dogmas and intuition, is sheer suicide. We must resign ourselves to the fact that there is no other fate for us than to climb the long, hard, steep and stony road guided by the only thing that makes us different from animals: reason.

We cannot be held back by certain traditions regarded as sacred. After all, what is tradition?

Sometimes we have to follow it for a century. Sometimes we have to create it to be followed by another century.

Sovereignty of the community and regulation of the interdependence of peoples in society by universal law are the two central pillars upon which the cathedral of democracy rests.

If we want to build this cathedral and live as free men in security, let us bear in mind the profound words of Francis Bacon in the *Novum Organum:*

It is idle to expect any great advancement in sciences from the superinducing and engrafting of new things upon old. We must begin anew from the very foundation, unless we would revolve forever in a circle with mean and contemptible progress.

It would be mean and contemptible progress indeed and we should be revolving in a circle if, instead of beginning to construct the new world society based on universal law, we again try to superinduce and engraft another league or council of sovereign nations upon the old.